# The Now and Zen Epicure

## Gourmet Cuisine for the Enlightened Palate

Miyoko Nishimoto

**Book Publishing Company**
Summertown, Tennessee

Cover design: Barbara McNew
Photography: Thomas Johns
Food Styling: Louise Hagler / Miyoko Nishimoto

*On the front cover, clockwise from upper left: Herb-Garlic Cheese Ball, pg. 33,
Pâté en Croûte, pgs. 42-3, Hot Herb Cheese Puffs, pg. 34, Spinach Napoleons,
pg. 56, Savory Stuffed Onions, pg. 29, Curried Mushroom Tarts, pg. 54*

*On the back cover, clockwise fron upper left: Vegetable Aspic Terrine, pgs. 44-5,
Greek Olive and Basil Mousse, pg. 58, Chocolate Almond Raspberry Torte, pgs.
204-5*

*Back cover quote by Cynthia Robbins--reprinted with permission from the San
Francisco Examiner.*
*© 1991  San Francisco Examiner*

Nishimoto, Miyoko, 1957-
       The now and Zen epicure : gourmet cuisine for the enlightened palate / by
Miyoko Nishimoto.
             p.              cm.
       Includes index.
       ISBN 0-913990-78-7
       1. Vegetarian cookery. 2. Cookery, Japanese. I. Title
TX837.N57  1991
641.5'636--dc20                                          91-13503
                                                              CIP

ISBN 0-913990-78-7

10 9 8 7 6 5 4 3 2

*Calculations for the nutritional analyses in this book are based on the average number
of servings listed with the recipes and the average amount of an ingredient if a range
is  called for. Calculations are rounded up to the nearest gram. If two options for an
ingredient are listed, the first one is used. Not included are fat used for frying, unless
the amount is specified in the  recipe, optional ingredients, or serving suggestions.*

The Book Publishing Company
PO Box 99
Summertown, TN 38483

# Contents

# PREFACE

I have met a few stoics in my life who ate mainly for sustenance, but I believe most of us have had a life-long love affair with food. My own interest began at the age of twelve when, for reasons not fully understood even to myself, I became a vegetarian. Our seventh grade class had gone on a camping trip. We had been divided into several food groups, in which we prepared our own meals. I got stuck in the vegetarian group with the teacher and the only two vegetarians in the class. I didn't know how I would manage to get through those three days without the meat I loved and thought necessary for stamina, but I kept thinking of it as an experiment and challenge, and thus survived. However, to my surprise, I was unable to eat the pork chops my mother placed in front of me for dinner when I returned home. I decided to give vegetarianism another week's try, again simply to see if I could make it.

Of course, my parents protested loudly. They were certain that their darling, albeit rebellious, daughter would die of malnutrition, and the arguments did not cease for several weeks. Finally, my mother, seeing my resolve and the fact that I was getting no skinnier, gave up arguing...as well as cooking for me. So, I was on my own. Armed with a few recipes from one of my vegetarian schoolmates (her whole family was vegetarian and had pictures of some guru hanging all over their house), I braved the pots and stove and diligently read Adele Davis to ensure that I was getting enough protein. Thus the experiments in cooking began.

It was the late sixties, so I made a lot of the "organic-type" food for which vegetarianism got a bad name—carob brownies, soy burgers, and lentil casseroles. It was good down-home food, but nothing fancy. Then, at a graduation party at Ernie's in San Francisco (the only time I have ever been to this fine restaurant), I was served a special vegetarian plate of the most deliciously prepared vegetables I have ever eaten. I discovered French cuisine, and spent the next few years at college reading Julia Child. Although I had adamantly refused to eat sugar as a vegetarian child, I began to use it freely, along with heavy cream, butter, rich cheeses, and refined flours. I threw fancy dinner parties. My roommates gladly let me have run of the kitchen. I was eating and serving wonderful things, but was probably no kinder to the body than the average meat eater.

I realized this several years later while living in Japan. I wanted to go back to a more natural diet, but did not want to sacrifice the richness and taste I had learned to love. There was no cookbook available that could show me how to do this as most gourmet vegetarian cookbooks relied heavily on dairy products and eggs. I had to set about experimenting all over again. Eventually, with the help of my ex-husband and friends who participated in weekly "taste-testing parties," I was able to develop a new and unique cuisine that allowed one to indulge while remaining perfectly healthy and completely vegetarian.

Many of the recipes in this book reflect this new cuisine. From them you can make delicious creations that will impress the fussiest dinner guest. He or she will never even think about whether it is vegetarian or not because the "good-for-you" food will be so good. So, throw away your fears about serving a somewhat offbeat dinner to your boss, because he will only be impressed by the wonderful things you set before him. I have fallen out of the habit of telling unsuspecting dinner guests that the fare they are about to be served is purely vegetarian. In many cases telling them is tantamount to giving them a warning:

BEWARE!
THE FOOD YOU ARE ABOUT TO BE SERVED
MAY ENDANGER YOUR PALATE.
EAT AT YOUR OWN RISK!

They will often be predisposed, and negatively, to the meal. So I suggest that you create one of the menus given in this book and serve it without any fanfare. Then sit back and listen to the "ooh's" and "aah's" as the guests marvel.

One of my greatest cooking influences has been Japanese

"Kaiseki" cuisine, a highly sophisticated and formal style of food with its cultural roots in Buddhism and tea ceremony. In Kaiseki cuisine, a wide array of beautifully arranged dishes is served in tiny portions over a range of courses called "mountain," "sea," "land," etc., denoting where the ingredients are from. Although I do not adhere to the true tenets of Kaiseki cuisine in my cooking, I have tried to simulate the atmosphere of it by devising menus and dishes that are served in small portions with numerous courses arranged to achieve a balance of flavors, colors, and textures. It is a fun way to eat and guests are always intrigued by what will come next. Unlike the American way of serving voluminous amounts of some main dish accompanied by a couple of side dishes, eating "Kaiseki style" will provide a unique dining experience for all.

People become vegetarians for a variety of reasons ranging from health considerations to environmental and humanitarian issues. The purpose of this book is not to convert everyone to vegetarianism, but simply to offer recipes for fine dining and home cooking. The emphasis here is on good taste and artful presentation because food is a celebration of life, not just sustenance for stoics. Food should nourish both the body and spirit. For it to nourish the former, it must please and satisfy the latter. Herein lies one of the key factors to good health. Relax. Enjoy. Moderation is the motto. Eat as naturally as you can, maintaining a low-fat diet rich in fiber and complex carbohydrates, but don't be afraid to indulge once in a while. A little rich food will occasionally do wonders for a person's soul, especially if they are the dishes in this book. The Greeks had a god of wine named Dionysus (Bacchus to the Romans) who punished those who were too strict with themselves and would not join in the revelry. So, don't be afraid. Go ahead and pour that libation to Dionysus. Then pour some for yourself and have it with something wonderful like French Moussaka, Pâté en Croûte, or Strawberry Almond Tart.

And many happy hours of discovery to you in the kitchen!

## Everything You
## Always Wanted to Know
## About Agar
## And Then Some:

## An Explanation
## Of Ingredients and Their Uses

AGAR, or "kanten" in Japanese, is a seaweed product that can replace gelatin in most recipes. Unlike gelatin, agar will set at room temperature in 30 to 60 minutes and become a bit firmer when refrigerated. It is available in bar, flake, or powdered forms. The bar form, which is the most prevalent in Japan, is the least processed. It can be found in Oriental food stores and some natural food stores; otherwise, the flakes or powder are more commonly found.

Unlike gelatin, agar will only set if it is completely dissolved by boiling or simmering. Lemon juice and ingredients containing oxalic acid (such as spinach) will require more than the usual amount of agar to set properly, although a small amount of lemon juice will not usually affect the setting ability. Although agar will never become rubbery like gelatin, too much of it will produce a very hard, unappetizing product. Thus the amount used is crucial to producing a dish with the proper texture and hardness. I have found that in mousses and bavarians where a delicate, gelatinous texture is desired, a combination of kanten and arrowroot (or better yet, "kuzu") produces a very similar effect.

Aside from its jelling powers, agar has many other uses. Cooked along with rice, it will provide a sheen and luscious texture and help to preserve it. It also lends a creamy texture when used in frozen desserts and ice cream. It has no calories and is among the highest in fiber of any plant product known.

Although the bar form has been used in most of the recipes in this book, the powdered or flake forms may be successfully and easily substituted:

1 teaspoon of agar powder = roughly one bar

1/4 cup of agar flakes = one teaspoon of powder or one bar

*Agar*

*Agar bars, powder and flakes*

However, depending on the ingredients being used, the amount of liquid and solid matter, and the degree of hardness desired, the amounts will seem to vary from recipe to recipe. If you find that a recipe is not hard enough or is too hard for you, simply increase or decrease the amount of agar the next time you use it. And be sure to follow the directions for dissolving kanten, as it will not set if it is not dissolved properly. It is actually a very simple process and one that will become second nature to you once you learn it; it is less tricky than gelatin.

## HOW TO USE AGAR

*Bar form:* Run the bar under cold water to moisten it. It will become soft and pliable. Soak it in a bowl of water for at least five minutes (longer if desired; up to 24 hours.) Remove from the water and squeeze to extract water. The longer you soak it, the softer and less solid it becomes, so if you have left it soaking for several hours, be sure you get all of the little pieces. Shred it into little pieces and add it to the liquid called for in the recipe. Bring it to a boil in a small saucepan, preferably covered, especially if only a small amount of liquid—a half cup or so—is being used. Lower the heat and stir frequently, letting it simmer on medium to medium-high heat for 2 to 3 minutes until it is completely dissolved. It must be added to the other ingredients in the recipe while it is still hot or it will set right there in the pan as it cools.

*Powder or flakes:* The soaking process can be skipped with these two forms, making it slightly less fussy to use. Otherwise, the directions are the same: add it to the liquid called for in the recipe, bring to a boil, covered, and then allow it to simmer on medium to medium-high heat for 2 to 3 minutes, stirring frequently.

When adding dissolved agar to the other ingredients in a recipe (as in mousses, terrines, bavarians, etc.), it is a good idea to add it while the blender or food processor is running. If it is not mixed or blended adequately, you will find little pieces of hardened agar in your creamy mousse, and this, to say the least, will not be pleasant. If you are not using a blender or food processor, add it in a steady stream while whisking rapidly and continuously so that it is uniformly incorporated.

A note on purchasing agar: The powder or flake forms can be extremely expensive if purchased in natural food stores, where they are not readily available. Japanese stores usually carry the bars at a more reasonable price. However, I have found some wholesale herb and spice distributors who sell the powdered or flaked variety by the pound at a much more reasonable price. If you plan to use a lot of it, as I do, it may be worthwhile to mail-order a pound from one of these sources (see source list at end of book.) Although you may initially have to shell out $18 to $20 for one pound, you will find that it goes a long way and you will have saved a considerable amount.

ARROWROOT is a substance that thickens like cornstarch. It is derived from the root of a plant that is considered highly nutritive. If a large quantity is used, it will produce a texture that is slightly more gelatinous than cornstarch. Arrowroot is available in natural food stores.

*Arrowroot*

CAROB, or St. John's Bread (this is what St. John supposedly ate in the woods), is a highly nutritious pod or bean that, when ground, becomes a cocoa-like substance and can be substituted for chocolate in most recipes. Although it looks and tastes like chocolate, it has less than half the fat of cocoa and contains no caffeine, theobromine, or oxalic acid, substances that can make chocolate undesirable for many people. Because of its naturally high sugar content (40%), carob desserts can be made with the addition of a minimum amount of sweetener. Cocoa, on the other hand, is extremely bitter if left unsweetened. Carob contains protein, B vitamins, and calcium, making it a very wholesome treat for young and old. Although some chocolate aficionados object to the more "homely" flavor of carob, I find that most people rarely know the difference if a carob dessert is prepared and flavored properly with the addition of natural grain coffee, vanilla, and/or various spirits or liqueurs.

*Carob*

Carob powder can be purchased either raw or lightly

toasted. The recipes in this book use the lightly toasted version, so if only the raw type is available, toast it by spreading it on a baking sheet and putting it in a low oven (150° F.) for ten to fifteen minutes, or you can dry-roast it in a skillet over a low flame. Be careful that it does not burn.

The block carob or carob chips that are available in some natural food stores can be used like chocolate bars or baking chocolate in most recipes. They may or may not be sweetened. Since carob is naturally sweet, I find that the unsweetened variety is preferable since it allows me to control the amount of additional sweetener in the recipe. If only the sweetened kind is available, check to see what sweetener has been used. Probably the healthiest types are those sweetened with date sugar or barley malt. Otherwise they may contain white or brown sugar, fructose, or corn syrup, which are less desirable. There is no carob equivalent to bittersweet or unsweetened baking chocolate because of carob's naturally high sugar content, but this does not usually pose a problem in most recipes where substitutions are made. Simply decrease the amount of sweetener called for if you are using carob in place of bitter baking chocolate. If block carob is unavailable, simply mix three tablespoons of carob powder in one tablespoon of water and two teaspoons of margarine, oil, or shortening for each 1 oz. square of chocolate or block carob.

Because the block carob contains palm or palm kernel oil, it is high in saturated fat and thus should not become an "everyday treat." I, however, see no reason not to indulge occasionally. Also, vegans should look for the dairy-free form which is available in most natural food stores. Carob chips can be used in the same way as block carob, and should be melted in a double boiler over low heat, as you would with chocolate. Be sure that all the utensils used with carob are completely dry since even a drop of water can cause the carob to become grainy. Should this happen, the addition of a tablespoon or two of vegetable shortening will restore its smoothness and meltability. Also, carob burns as easily as chocolate and will refuse to melt if the heat is too high. If you find this to be a problem, turn off the heat and let it sit for awhile over hot water, stirring occasionally.

COCONUT MILK can easily be made at home by blending hot water with grated, unsweetened coconut. Combine grated, shredded, or flaked coconut with twice the amount of boiling water (in volume, not weight) in the blender and whip for three or four minutes. Strain through cheesecloth or a fine wire mesh, pressing as much milk out of the pulp as possible. The amount of hot water can be increased or decreased according to the consistency of the milk or "cream" desired. Coconut milk can give a tropical flair to drinks, desserts, ice creams and cakes, and can lend a wonderful depth and subtle sweetness to curries. Unfortunately, it, too, is high in saturated fats and thus should not become a daily part of the diet.

*Coconut Milk*

KUZU-KO OR KUDZU is a high quality starch or thickening agent derived from the root of the kuzu plant which has been touted for its medicinal powers in the Orient for ages. It comes in small rock-like pieces which dissolve easily in water. Although it is used like arrowroot or cornstarch, much less is needed to thicken and bind; use only half the amount called for. Unlike cornstarch and other highly refined starches, kuzu-ko is is natural and unprocessed.

*Kuzu*

Although kuzu is more expensive than cornstarch or arrowroot, I prefer the smooth and subtle texture it lends to mousses and other dishes; arrowroot can become too gelatinous.

MIRIN is a sweet Japanese sake (rice wine) that is often used in cooking to add a sweetness, roundness, or mellowness to a dish. Because it is an alcoholic substance, it will evaporate entirely in cooking, leaving only its flavor. Although it was originally made from only glutinous sweet rice and "kohji" (an enzyme used in the fermentation of sake and miso), mass production has introduced the use of sugar, distilled alcohol, and sometimes dextrose or other starches as ingredients to expedite the fermentation and production. The alcoholic content can be an indication of how natural the product is;

*Mirin*

the higher the content (10%-12%), the "truer" it probably is. Mirin that contains sugar and other ingredients will only have a minimal alcoholic content (2%-3%). Reading the label closely will help you select a natural brand, but mirin is used in such small quantities that even the less pure types are acceptable. Natural or Oriental food stores and even some supermarkets stock mirin.

**Miso**

MISO is a fermented paste made primarily from soybeans, salt, and "kohji." It can also be made from rice, barley, or other grains and beans, and will vary greatly in flavor and character according to the substance used. It is a "living" product full of enzymes and friendly bacteria that aid digestion and keep the colon happy. In fact, the Japanese Ministry of Health and Welfare advises the Japanese to drink a bowl of miso soup daily for this reason. Traditionally, a day in Japan started with a bowl of this simple brew.

Although miso has been an integral part of Japanese cuisine for centuries, I find that it adapts easily to Western cooking, adding depth and flavor to many vegetarian dishes. Miso comes in various colors or grades of darkness; the lighter, golden-colored ones have a milder, less salty taste, and the dark brown variety has a saltier, more prominent flavor. I prefer a mellow, reddish-brown type called "sweet kohji miso" which I find to be neither too salty nor light in flavor. There are as many varieties of miso as wine, and each family in Japan will usually subscribe to a particular brand that they like. Oriental markets carry a fair selection. You may have to try several kinds before finding one that you like. The type of miso you incorporate in your recipes is not so crucial if you're using it in place of salt or as a flavoring, and not as the main ingredient in miso soup. Simply choose one that is neither too light nor dark in color. The grains or beans used to make the miso will affect its flavor, with barley or barley mixtures considered the tastiest by some. But here again, I find that all of this depends on the length of time the miso was allowed to ferment, its salt content, and other factors peculiar to each manufacturer, making even the same "type" of miso widely varying in flavor.

Like peanut butter, miso comes in both "smooth" and "chunky" styles. Both are acceptable in miso soup, although the former is better for flavoring most dishes. (Speaking of peanut butter, I once had an American friend in Tokyo who told me of all the huge vats of peanut butter in his local supermarket. I told him they probably contained miso. Undeterred, he bought himself a pound of it, and later told me about his very salty peanut butter-and-jelly sandwich!)

Aside from the recipes in this book that use miso as a flavoring agent, do go ahead and try it in place of salt in spaghetti or tomato sauces, stir-fried vegetables, and casseroles; you will find it lends a meaty and satisfying depth to your cooking.

NUT MILKS made from cashews, almonds, or sesame seeds can be a tasty and nutritious substitute for dairy or soy milk in cooking. They are easily made by blending blanched raw nuts with water in a blender or food processor. Although nuts are high in fat, they are also high in magnesium, calcium, and other valuable minerals, and can lend a richness and depth to many dishes and sauces. The Chinese have a delicious custard-like dessert made from almond milk that has a subtle sweetness and flavor that can not be achieved with either dairy or soy milk. This book contains many recipes that call for either cashew or almond milk.

*Nut Milks*

To make cashew milk, combine 1/4 to 1/3 cup cashews with 1 cup of water in a blender for 2 to 3 minutes until absolutely smooth. Straining is not necessary. For almond milk, start with blanched almonds (you can remove the skins by plunging the whole, raw almonds in boiling water for a few minutes. The skins will slip off easily.) Follow the directions for cashew milk, but strain it to remove the remaining pulp since almonds are harder nuts than cashews.

*Cashew Milk*

*Almond Milk*

Hulled sesame seeds are used to make milk in the same way.

The proportion of nuts to water can be increased to produce a richer milk or NUT CREAM. Add as much as you want to achieve the desired thickness. Brazil nuts are excel-

*Nut Cream*

lent as a rich cream, as are cashews, and both can be flavored with honey, vanilla, or a liqueur to produce a delicious dessert topping or sauce.

**Nutritional Yeast**

NUTRITIONAL YEAST is a vitamin- and mineral-packed food substance that is available in flake or powder forms in natural food stores. Unlike brewer's yeast, which is almost offensive in flavor, nutritional yeast is delicious. It adds great fullness, richness, and depth if used in combination with other ingredients, and is thus used profusely throughout this book.

**Okara**

OKARA is the leftover pulp of the soybean that results from making soy milk or tofu. It is thus the "other half" of the soy bean, containing all its fiber and a considerable amount of protein, while being much lower in fat than tofu. It is a white, fluffy, moist substance that, despite its nutritional value, is so lacking in flavor that 99.9% of the okara produced in Japan is either fed to hogs or used as fertilizer. Although tons of it are produced daily, it is rarely available to consumers in Japan; one has to arrive at a neighborhood tofu shop practically at dawn to get any before it is all carted away. I have had to run around to 6 or 7 shops before finding one that had kept even a pound or two for sale.

In all the centuries of tofu production in Japan, okara has traditionally been used in basically one dish called "U No Hana," a tasty blend of vegetables and okara seasoned with soy sauce, mirin, and stock. However, it is a versatile ingredient that can be used to bind or fill croquettes, dumplings, nut or bean loaves, or used to replace some of the flour in cakes and pastries.

If you make your own tofu and end up with mounds of okara and do not know what to do with it, try adding it to burgers and loaves. Or you can partly dry it in a non-stick frying pan over low heat, stirring almost constantly, and use it in cakes or cookies, or to replace breadcrumbs in coating croquettes for frying. Cookies made with okara do tend to absorb a lot of moisture, so it is best to use it in a "soft-type" cookie.

To make semi-dried okara, place it in a dry skillet and cook over very lowheat, stirring almost constantly, until most of the moisture evaporates and it looks fluffy, light, and does not clump up. As it dries, it will increase in volume; to get 1 cup of dried okara start with 1/2 to 2/3 cup wet okara. It should take about 10-15 minutes to dry in a skillet.

Dried okara can be purchased by mail. Write:

> Now and Zen
> P.O. Box 591614
> San Francisco, CA 94118

SAKE, or Japanese rice wine, is as wonderful to drink on a nippy winter night as it is to use in cooking. It is used extensively in Japanese cuisine and in several recipes in this book. Sake comes in various grades, and a dry sake is preferable to a sweet one for both cooking and drinking. In cooking, dry sherry or a dry vermouth can be substituted if sake is not available.

*Sake*

If you are going to drink the sake, warm it up by pouring it into a small ceramic pitcher or bottle and place in simmering water for a few minutes. Do not let the sake boil—it should be hot but not scalding. Enjoy!

SHIMEJI, or oyster mushrooms, grow in clumps and have a delicate texture and flavor. They can be found in Japanese food stores as well as some supermarkets. Although more expensive than regular button mushrooms, they can add a wonderful contrast and flavor to many dishes.

*Shimeji, or oyster mushrooms*

SHIITAKE, or black mushrooms, are perhaps the best known of all Oriental mushrooms and are used extensively in both Chinese and Japanese cooking. They have a rich, deep, meaty flavor and texture and lend themselves well to everything from stocks to being stuffed as an appetizer. They are available either fresh or dried and in either case will be very expensive if purchased in a natural food store or supermarket. If there is a Chinatown or Chinese market where you live, it is definitely worth a trip to purchase a pound bag of dried shiitake mushrooms, since they will be

*Shiitake mushrooms*

considerably less expensive. Although a few dishes call for fresh shiitake mushrooms, you'll get better results with the dried ones which are meatier and more flavorful. They are also high in vitamin D and have been used as an ingredient in Chinese herbal therapy for centuries.

The best method for reconstituting dried mushrooms is soaking in tepid water for a couple of hours; this gives you a nice stock from the soaking water that can be used to flavor Oriental dishes such as stir-fry vegetables and sauce. If you are pressed for time, the soaking can be expedited by using hot water but the resulting stock will not be as flavorful. As the mushrooms vary in size, it is hard to give the exact amount of water to use, but two to four mushrooms per cup of water should reconstitute the mushrooms and yield a flavorful stock. I find it helpful to keep a large jar of mushrooms soaking in liquid in the refrigerator, so I can use them anytime. They will keep for a week or two under refrigeration.

Once again, shiitake mushrooms come in various grades with the thick "donkoh shiitake" being the best variety. When buying dried shiitake, try to find ones that are thick with a crinkled, cracked surface; they will be much more flavorful. In fact, a good shiitake mushroom is so good that a light grilling or sauteing with soy sauce and lemon juice is all that it needs.

*Soy Milk*

SOY MILK: There are so many varieties of soy milk on the natural food market today that it both baffles and delights someone like myself who has had to make it from scratch most of her life. Soy milk—and very good soy milk—can be made at home fairly easily, but there are a number of acceptable brands on the market today. What one wants to avoid with soy milk is the "beany" taste. A number of commercial brands have managed to eliminate this with a minimum of adulteration. Some have added oil to produce a rich and creamy product suitable for use as "cream" or half-and-half in dairy free recipes. Others have blended in "kombu" (a type of seaweed) and barley malt to produce a lighter, though still creamy, tasty product. Some brands of soy milk now come in aseptic packaging, allowing you to store it without refrigeration. Chinese and Japanese food stores also carry soy milk, but be sure to purchase a brand that does not contain sugar. If you are using pure, unblended soy milk made from only soybeans and water, you can eliminate the beany taste by adding a very small amount of salt and maple syrup or honey. This gives it a creamier consistency, especially if the soy milk is thick rather than thin and watery.

A slightly richer "SOY CREAM" can be produced by blending in two to three tablespoons of oil per cup of unblended soy milk, along with the tiny amount of salt and sweetener. If you want to keep your fat intake to a minimum, use a commercial, blended brand that does not contain any additional oil.

*Soy Cream*

SOY SAUCE has become a household word in America, although I remember a time when the only soy sauce available was a strange, sweet and salty substance with caramel coloring that came on your table in Chinese restaurants. Today, many fine brands are available in not only natural and Oriental food stores, but supermarkets as well. A gallon can will be considerably cheaper than little bottles, and you will find that it is an indispensable ingredient in many of the recipes in this book. Soy sauce can be used in place of salt in soups, sauces, casseroles, and other dishes (Western as well as Oriental) and will not be overpowering in flavor.

*Soy sauce*

There are many brands of soy sauce. The best contain only soy beans, salt, and wheat, and have been aged slowly. They will be rich and deep in color and absolutely delicious over chilled fresh tofu with grated ginger and green onions. But here again, as with miso, soy sauce manufacturers have compromised quality for quantity, and often use alcohol, sugar, caramel coloring, and monosodium glutamate to approximate a true soy sauce. Read the label.

SOY SOUR CREAM, or a soy substitute for sour cream, is easily made by draining soy yogurt (see recipe for Soy Yogurt that follows). Place the yogurt in a bag made of cheesecloth or gauze, and hang it above the kitchen sink to

*Soy sour cream*

drain until you have a thick, creamy substance (several hours or overnight.) Or, line a colander with a double thickness of cheesecloth and drain the yogurt in that. A little salt and lemon juice will counteract the beany taste while bringing out the sourness. Although tofu "sour cream" (see recipe on page 179) can be used in dips and toppings, soy sour cream made from soy yogurt is more effective when the richness of sour cream is desired in dishes like Curried Stuffed Zucchini Boats, page 126.

*Soy yogurt*

SOY YOGURT is as easily made as dairy yogurt and can be extremely thick, rich and sweet. You simply add a culture (either acidophilus or a few tablespoons of a commercial dairy yogurt) to warm soy milk and let it sit in a warm place until it sets in a few hours. Heat a quart of soy milk until it feels warm to your wrist. Mix in two to three tablespoons of a commercial plain yogurt (use only "real" yogurt made from milk and culture; it should not contain gelatin, stabilizers, sugar, or other ingredients.) You may want to mix the commercial yogurt with a small amount of the warm soy milk first to make it easier to mix in. Cover, set it in a warm place, and do not disturb for 3 to 5 hours. It should set nicely. If it does not set, the temperature of the soy milk may have been too high and the culture killed; or you may not have set it in a warm enough place. Some recipes suggest keeping the temperature of the milk at around 110°. I have never bothered to use a thermometer and have rarely had trouble with yogurt not setting properly. There are really no mysteries to making it.

The Egyptian cook for a family, with whom I stayed in Cairo, once used to pour his yogurt in jars then wrap them with towels and set them on the kitchen counter, and it worked every time. I've had success wrapping the jars or containers in down jackets or blankets to enclose the heat. Anywhere with a pilot light, a tub filled with lukewarm water, near a radiator, heater, or fireplace, or a conventional or microwave oven with a "warm" setting can be used to set the yogurt. Look around and you will find an appropriate place in your house.

If you are going to eat it as yogurt, refrigerate it overnight first; it will get thicker and tastier as it chills. If you are using it for sour cream, it can be drained right away (see instructions on pages 11 and 12).

*Tahini*

TAHINI, or sesame paste or butter, has been a staple in the Middle East and Orient for ages. It is rich and flavorful, and contains a high level of calcium in an easily digestible form. It can be used to make spreads, sauces, dips, baked goods, desserts, and can act as a binder to replace eggs in many dishes. Several natural food manufacturers produce tahini today, and it varies greatly in flavor and texture. For the recipes in this book, it is best to use a silky, smooth type that uses lightly toasted hulled white sesame seeds (some tahinis are grainier than others).

*Tamari*

TAMARI is a soy sauce-like brew made from soybeans only and contains no wheat. It has become popular in the United States recently because it is lower in sodium than soy sauce and has a deep rich flavor. However, tamari accounts for less than 1% of all soy sauce production in Japan, and most of that is exported to the United States. It is also more expensive than soy sauce. Tamari can be used in place of soy sauce in any of the recipes in this book. It is also a perfect substitute for those on a wheat-free diet.

*Tempeh*

TEMPEH is a cultured soy product that has been the mainstay of the Indonesian diet for centuries. Unlike tofu which is made from soy milk and thus contains no fiber, tempeh is produced from the entire bean. An edible mold is grown on partially cooked soy beans, forming a dense and easily digestible cake that can be prepared in a variety of ways. Tempeh can be baked, broiled, stewed, marinated, fried, sauteed, and steamed. Crumbled, it is a substitute for ground meat. It is available frozen in natural food stores.

Although it was once thought that all tempeh contained substantial amounts of vitamin B12, a vitamin that is not generally present in a pure vegetarian diet, it has now been found that the sterile manufacturing methods employed in the United States do not yield the bacteria that contains B12. However, tempeh is still an extremely nutritious soy product in an easily digestible form. Tempeh is highly perishable and should be refrigerated or frozen. If the recipe you're using does not indicate that the tempeh should be cooked in some manner for at least 15 minutes, steam or simmer for at least that long before using.

*Tofu*

TOFU, which was regarded in America a few years ago as a tasteless, white, soft substance, has become a rather celebrated food as of late. I have encountered so many different types of tofu recently that I feel I should write at least a short exposition on the matter to clear up what I find to be a rather confusing array of white blocks in water.

Tofu (soy bean curd) is made by adding a coagulant to soy milk, usually calcium sulfate or the more traditional magnesium chloride ("nigari" in Japanese), a mineral extracted from salt. The curds are then separated from the whey and pressed into a block. Various degrees of pressure are applied to produce different degrees of firmness. Japanese tofu, or what is sometimes called "regular tofu," is softer than Chinese tofu, which is often labeled "firm tofu." However, I have often bought a package of each by the same manufacturer and found them to be exactly the same. Other times, I would find that they varied greatly. Unless you find a brand that is consistent, the directions for pressing your own tofu given here should be followed in order to ensure uniformity in cooking each time. If the recipe simply calls for "tofu" and it does not specify "firm," "pressed," or "well drained," assume that it is the Japanese or "regular" type. This type is usually found in plastic containers holding about a pound, or it is sometimes sold in bulk in large buckets of water. There is another type that comes vacuum-packed that is much firmer than the regular type. It is similar to pressed Chinese tofu, found in Chinese groceries, and does not need to be drained or pressed before using in recipes that call for such. This very firm type is excellent for slicing or crumbling and sautéing. The "regular" type is better for blending in sauces, dips, and dessert toppings.

Another type, "silken tofu," is extremely smooth, delicate and soft. It may be packaged in plastic containers with water or in an aseptic carton that can be kept at room temperature for several months, making it a very convenient food item. Silken tofu is excellent in dishes where texture is of primary importance.

In Japan almost every neighborhood has a local tofu shop that makes batches of fresh tofu every morning. Tofu sellers also come by on bicycles blowing their distinctive sounding horn to inform housewives of their approach. But the purity and quality of tofu has fallen greatly in recent years. Originally tofu contained only whole soybeans, water, and "nigari." Calcium sulfate has largely replaced nigari now, and fillers and preservatives have been pumped into it. Whereas traditional Japanese tofu was a solid substance with a fresh, beany taste, most tofu today is watery and bland by comparison. Unfortunately, very few Japanese today have tasted truly delicious tofu. Perhaps this accounts for the decline in tofu consumption. Although America seems to carry a wider array of tofu that does not contain the unnecessary extras, a consumer should still read the labels and select as natural a brand as possible.

Freshness is crucial to tofu and can affect the flavor greatly. Tofu should have a clean, fresh smell and flavor; if it has a sharp, biting smell or taste, it has gone bad. Tofu that is to be used raw in recipes like mousses and puddings must be absolutely fresh. If you must use tofu that has a slight smell, boil it for five minutes before using, or better yet, turn it into frozen tofu (see below). The flavor, however, will never compare to fresh tofu. Unfortunately, tofu in America can sit on the shelf for several days, so check the date on it before buying.

FROZEN TOFU: Freezing tofu will entirely change the texture to yield a meaty, chewy substance that will soak up marinades and flavorings, and perform as a convincing meat substitute in many recipes. Since it defrosts in less than fifteen minutes and can be used immediately, it is a good idea to have a stock of it in the freezer at all times.

*Frozen tofu*

The texture and consistency of frozen tofu seems to vary with the type and brand, and you may have to experiment a little to find one that is the most chewy or "meaty." Generally speaking, however, the best frozen tofu is made from the firmer types, although any type (except silken) can be used. Again, there is a time factor involved; the tofu seems to get more chewy and "meaty" the longer it is frozen. Since this is the case, I recommend freezing it for at least one week, if not longer, before using (up to a year is alright).

To freeze tofu, remove it from its package, wrap in plastic wrap, and place in the freezer. To defrost, unwrap and place in hot or boiling water, changing the water as necessary. This will take anywhere from 5 to 25 minutes, depending on the amount you are defrosting, or you can defrost in a microwave. If you have all day, the tofu can thaw at room temperature. Before using, squeeze out all the water. The tofu will become considerably lighter and will resemble an old yellow sponge.

*Pressed tofu*

PRESSED OR WELL DRAINED TOFU: Some recipes call for a very firm tofu. Vacuum-packed brands are usually pressed hard and can be used as is in such recipes. Chinese grocers usually carry small squares of a dense tofu that has also been pressed, and these can be used as is. In the absence of these, it is very easy to press or drain your own tofu. Wrap the regular tofu (or even the so-called "firm" type that is packed in water) in a thick towel and allow it to drain in the refrigerator overnight. In the morning, the towel will be wet from the moisture of the tofu, and the tofu will be firm and dense. It can now be used.

Recipes in this book calling for this extra-firm pressed or drained tofu will give two quantities, the first for the amount of regular or water-packed "firm" tofu to start with if you are going to press or drain it yourself. The second quantity will read "pre-pressed." This will indicate the amount of extra firm vacuum-packed or dense Chinese-style tofu to use as is. (Example: 12-14 oz. tofu, pressed, or 8 oz. pre-pressed tofu.)

# Tiny Treasures

## Savory Mousses, Pâtés, Terrines, Tarts, and Other Wonderful Appetizers and Hors d'Ouevres

This is where the magic begins. Whether what follows is just a bowl of soup or a complicated multi-course affair, the first course will set the mood for the evening. By taking the time to make and serve an appetizer, you will make the simplest meal seem more elegant, and your guests will reward you well with their appreciation. Because appetizers are something "extra," like dessert, I think of them as very special, and I have a great deal of fun making fancy little tarts, beautifully molded mousses, and other delightful things. I know it will put everybody in the mood and perhaps ease any tension that may be in the air about "vegetarian food." There are many wonderful and unusual creations here, and your guests will delight in new flavors and textures.

You will find among these recipes dishes that are appropriate for fancy sit-down affairs, as well as pâtés and terrines for entertaining large parties or crowds. You can even make an entire meal from appetizers alone, serving an array of them, and forget the main course entirely. Most of these dishes can be prepared hours, or even days, in advance, giving you more time to enjoy your guests.

Just remember that an appetizer is something to whet the appetite and thus should not be too large. Be as decorative as possible, arranging and styling the treats as beautifully as you can.

Some of the recipes, such as the quiches or the Mediterranean Stuffed Tomatoes, can be served as a light main course. Others, like the pâtés, are wonderful to have on hand in the refrigerator in case friends drop in or just when the mood strikes.

# Mediterranean Stuffed Tomatoes

*Serves 8*

12 oz. regular tofu
    *or 8 oz. pressed tofu*

1/2 tsp. salt

1 cup parsley

2 - 3 Tbsp. capers

1 - 2 cloves garlic

1/4 cup good olive oil
    *(use extra-virgin if possible)*

2 Tbsp. lemon juice

1/2 cup walnuts

salt to taste

8 small or 4 large tomatoes
    *(must be very ripe)*

*Ripe tomatoes stuffed with tofu "cheese," walnuts, and a pungent sauce made from parsley, capers and garlic evoke images of islands and sun. Serve well-chilled on a hot summer evening.*

If you are using regular tofu, follow the instructions on page 28 for removing the water. Crumble and place in a non-stick frying pan with the salt. Do not add any oil to the pan. Over very low heat, dry-fry the tofu, stirring almost constantly, until it resembles dry cottage cheese. Do not allow it to burn or brown. This may take fifteen minutes. Allow to cool while making the green sauce.

Finely mince the parsley, capers, and garlic, and place in a mortar, "suribachi" (a Japanese mortar with grooves), or blender. If you are using a mortar and pestle or suribachi, grind the ingredients to a rough paste while adding the olive oil, one tablespoon at a time. Add the lemon juice last. If using a blender, add two tablespoons of the olive oil, blend for fifteen seconds, then add the rest and blend for another five or ten. Do not allow it to become a homogeneous mass because some texture is important to this sauce. Mix in the lemon juice by hand.

Chop the walnuts and mix with the tofu and the sauce. Add salt if necessary.

Cut the tops off the tomatoes. Trim the bottoms slightly so that they stand and do not roll over. Remove the insides of the tomatoes, leaving a wall 1/3" thick—the insides can be used for making tomato sauce. Fill with the tofu mixture and chill three to four hours before serving. This dish should be made the day you are going to serve it, since the parsley will lose its wonderful bright green color if allowed to stand too long.

Serve on a bed of lettuce or other greens.

*Per serving: Calories: 174, Protein: 7 gm., Fat: 7 gm., Carbohydrates: 9 gm.*

# Caponata

*This is a wonderful medley of eggplants, peppers, and tomatoes, similar to ratatouille but with a sweet and sour touch. It is best served cold or at room temperature and keeps splendidly in the refrigerator for a week or two. Serve as part of a cold plate or a salad on a bed of greens. I like to mound it on leaves of Belgian endive and serve it along with the preceding Mediterranean Stuffed Tomatoes.*

Cut the eggplant into 3/4" cubes, salt lightly, and place in a colander to drain for half an hour. Rinse and squeeze gently or pat dry with paper towels.

Mince the garlic and cut the peppers into rings or large chunks. Heat the olive oil in a large pan or wok and sauté the onions until they begin to wilt. Add the eggplant and continue to sauté for five to ten minutes, or until relatively soft. Add the tomatoes and peppers and continue cooking for another ten minutes. Then add all the remaining ingredients except the pine nuts, cover, and cook fifteen minutes.

Toast the pine nuts in an oven until golden brown, taking care not to let them burn. Add to the vegetables and allow the entire dish to cool. If possible, wait a day before serving as the flavor improves and mellows. If too sweet, add a dash more vinegar; if not sweet enough, add a touch more honey. Season with salt and pepper to taste.

*Per serving: Calories: 212, Protein: 6 gm., Fat: 8 gm., Carbohydrates: 21 gm.*

Serves 6

18 oz. eggplant
  (either American or Japanese)

3 - 4 cloves garlic

2 green peppers,
  or 1 green and 1 red or yellow

3 Tbsp. olive oil

1 1/2 medium onions, sliced

1 1/4 lbs. ripe tomatoes
  (use canned if they are not
  really ripe and juicy)

1 tsp. salt

3 Tbsp. capers

3 Tbsp. tomato paste

1/2 cup parsley, chopped

2 tsp. dried basil
  or 1/4 cup finely chopped fresh
  basil

3 1/2 Tbsp. red wine vinegar

1 Tbsp. honey

1/2 cup pine nuts

salt and freshly ground pepper to
  taste

# Eggplant Salad

*Serves 6*

1 large eggplant (about 1 1/4 lbs.)

1 tomato, chopped

1/2 medium onion, minced

2 large cloves garlic, minced

1/2 Tbsp. soy sauce

1 Tbsp. olive oil

2 Tbsp. red wine vinegar

1/2 tsp. crushed red pepper

salt and pepper to taste

3 Tbsp. parsley, minced

*This works either as a salad on a bed of greens surrounded by olives or marinated artichoke hearts, or as a dip or spread for crackers or bread.*

Bake eggplant for 20 to 25 minutes at 375° or until very soft. Allow to cool. Peel off the skin or split in two and scoop out the pulp. Discard the skin unless you like a slightly burnt taste—some do. Place the eggplant in a bowl and mix with the other ingredients. Refrigerate overnight or at least 5 hours before serving to allow flavors to mingle.

*Per serving: Calories: 56, Protein: 2 gm., Fat: 0 gm., Carbohydrates: 8 gm.*

# Savory Stuffed Onions

*People always ask what these are made of. It's obvious that the shell is a well-baked onion, but the delectable mixture inside keeps everyone guessing. The preliminary steaming and final baking bring out the sweetness of the onions, harmonizing beautifully with the slightly "meaty" filling. Cutting up all these raw onions may leave you crying, but this dish is worth the tears. Use the smallest onions you can find, preparing one per person, or cut larger ones in half and serve one-half each.*

If you are using small onions, cut a slice off the top and bottom of each so they sit up. If you are using large onions, cut each in half horizontally, as for onion rings, then slice a bit off the bottom so that each half sits up. Using a melon scooper or a sharp-edged measuring spoon, scoop out the insides of the onions, leaving a wall 1/4" to 1/3" thick (2 to 3 layers, depending on their size). Mince the onion pulp and set aside for later. Steam or microwave the onion shells until they are soft but still retain their shape.

Sauté the minced onions in 2 tablespoons of the margarine. Finely grind the cashews in a blender. Mix the onions, cashews, breadcrumbs, parsley, and sage, and moisten with two to three tablespoons of soy milk. Season with salt and pepper to taste. Stuff the steamed onions with this mixture, then melt the remaining tablespoon of margarine and pour a little on top of each. Bake at 350° until golden brown, about 15 to 25 minutes, depending on the onions' size. Serve hot.

*Per serving: Calories: 170, Protein: 5 gm., Fat: 6 gm., Carbohydrates: 19 gm.*

*Serves 8*

*See photo on front cover.*

*8 small or 4 large onions*

*3 Tbsp. margarine*

*1/2 cup raw cashews*

*1 cup fresh breadcrumbs
(preferably whole wheat—
white will do, while darker
breads such as rye and pum-
pernickel are not suitable)*

*1/3 cup parsley, chopped*

*1/2 tsp. rubbed sage*

*2 - 3 Tbsp. soy milk*

# Zucchini, Eggplant and Fennel Filling

Serves 4-8

*This unusual and tasty filling can go in all sorts of stuffable items. Be creative with the "containers," keeping in mind what else you are serving for the meal. It makes a wonderful filling for baked onions (see recipe for Savory Stuffed Onions, page 116), but it is also nice in tarts, sandwiched between puff pastry layers, or wrapped in crêpes. These would be nice additions to a hot appetizer tray.*

shells of your choice
   (such as pre-baked tart shells,
   puff pastry, crêpes, and giant
   mushrooms)
1 lb. (medium) eggplant
2 medium zucchini
1 tsp. salt
2 medium onions
2 Tbsp. olive oil
2 cups lightly packed fennel tops,
   chopped (the feathery part)
5 - 6 Tbsp. tomato paste
salt and pepper to taste

This recipe makes enough filling for about 12 mushrooms, 8 small onions, 4-8 crêpes, 4-8 individual tarts, or 20-25 canapés. If you select small onions as the shells for this filling, you may use the insides you'll remove instead of the 2 onions listed in the recipe. Refer to the recipe for Savory Stuffed Onions on page 116 for directions on preparing onions for filling.

Bake the eggplants at 300° for about 40 minutes until soft and a fork pierces through easily. Allow to cool, then remove the skin and mash the pulp. Grate the zucchini and place in a colander. Sprinkle with a teaspoon of salt and allow to drain for twenty minutes. Squeeze out the excess liquid.

Chop the onions, or onion pulp if you are stuffing onions. Sauté until tender in the olive oil, then add the zucchini and cook a few more minutes until the zucchini is soft. Add the eggplant pulp and chopped fennel tops, and sauté another minute or two. Add the tomato paste and season to taste with salt and pepper while continuing to sauté for another two to three minutes to blend flavors.

Fill shells and bake in a moderate oven (350° - 375°) until piping hot, about 15 minutes.

*Per serving: Calories: 110, Protein: 3 gm., Fat: 1 gm., Carbohydrates: 16 gm.*

# Stuffed Shiitake Mushrooms

*Serves 4-8*

*Here is something to serve the skeptical non-vegetarian guest. The frozen tofu takes on the texture of meat and the ground walnuts add richness. These can be made a day or two in advance, and baked before serving time, or even baked several hours in advance and re-heated or served at room temperature. If you can get shiso leaves from a Japanese grocery store, place them under the mushrooms, as they not only look pretty but can be eaten—a delicious experience!*

Defrost the tofu as described on page 23, squeeze dry, and crumble. Sauté the onion and garlic in the olive oil until tender. Add the finely crumbled tofu and sauté another five minutes. Add the chopped tomato and the rosemary, and continue cooking for ten minutes until the flavors meld and the mixture is fairly dry. Add the ground walnuts, miso, tomato paste, salt and pepper to taste, and an additional few drops of olive oil if the mixture seems dry.

Cut off the stems from the shiitake mushrooms and mound the mixture into it with a spoon, pressing firmly with the inside of the spoon to form a smooth mound. Bake at 350° for 15 to 20 minutes until browned. Place on a shiso leaf and serve either hot or at room temperature.

*Per serving: Calories: 183, Protein: 9 gm., Fat: 9 gm., Carbohydrates: 7 gm.*

*12 - 14 oz. tofu, frozen*
*(see Frozen Tofu, page 23)*

*8 to 10 large shiitake mushrooms, fresh, or dried and soaked*

*1 medium onion, chopped*

*1 large clove garlic*

*2 Tbsp. olive oil*

*1 tomato, chopped*

*1/2 tsp. rosemary*

*1/3 cup ground walnuts*

*2 tsp. miso*

*2 Tbsp. tomato paste*

*salt and pepper to taste*

*8 - 10 shiso leaves (optional)*

# Tofu "Cheese"

*Makes 1 - 1 1/2 cups*

10 - 12 oz. well-pressed tofu

1 cup miso

1/2 cup white wine

1/4 cup (or more) mirin

*Tofu transforms into a smooth, spreadable, cheese-like substance when "pickled" in a mixture of miso, wine, and mirin. Miso alone will do the trick, but will produce a very salty cheese. Tofu cheese has many uses, the most delightful being my mock "boursin," the French herb-and-garlic cheese. It is also used in making an eggless version of aïoli, the sticky, garlicky, wonderful French mayonnaise that can be added to soups or can serve as a dip or sauce. It can be mixed into white sauces and dressings to lend a cheesy flavor or soaked in olive oil to become "feta" cheese. It will not, however, melt like mozzarella on a pizza.*

*It is crucial to use a mild miso. Use a light-colored, "sweet koji" miso if available. The quantity of wine and mirin will vary slightly with the saltiness of the miso, so it is hard to give exact quantities in the recipe. When you find a miso that seems to work well for this, stick with it so you can always be sure of the proportion of miso to wine and mirin. It is not absolutely vital to use an exact ratio and there is quite a bit of leeway that will produce "cheese."*

If you are pressing the tofu yourself, start with 1 lb. and follow the instructions on page 16.

Mix the miso, wine, and mirin to produce a slightly sweet but salty flavor. The consistency should be like a very thick salad dressing or light mayonnaise.

Slice the tofu 1/2" thick lengthwise. Wrap each piece in cheesecloth. Place in a container with the miso so that each slice is covered on all sides with the mixture. Cover and refrigerate for one week. After that time remove the tofu from the miso, take off the cheesecloth and check the consistency. It should be like a soft cream cheese and it may have taken on a light, yellowish-brown hue. If it does not spread smoothly like cream cheese, you may have added too much wine, and will have to put it back in the miso mixture for another day or two. If you use only miso and no wine or mirin, this process will take only 24 to 36 hours to become "cheese." Use as desired in the recipes on pages 33 - 35. This keeps in the refrigerator for one to two weeks.

*Per 2 Tbsp. serving: Calories: 57, Protein: 3 gm., Fat: 1 gm., Carbohydrates: 8 gm.*

# Tofu "Boursin" Or Herb-Garlic Cheese Ball

*I make no claims for this being low in fat or calories but it is dairy-free and absolutely wonderful. This tastes so much like real cheese that I fooled a group of unsuspecting French friends with it.*

Combine the tofu, dried herbs, lemon juice, garlic, and margarine in a food processor or blender and whiz until very smooth and homogenized. The amount of margarine will vary slightly each time with the moisture content of the tofu. Add enough to make it smooth. Finally, add the fresh herbs and blend for another moment. Transfer to a bowl and refrigerate several hours or overnight until firm enough to mold. In warm weather you may have to freeze it for thirty minutes or so before being able to mold it into a ball. Roll it in the chopped nuts and serve with thin slices of bread or crackers, or just pack it a bowl and serve as is.

This can also be used for Hot Herb Cheese Puffs on page 34.

*Per 1 Tbsp. serving: Calories: 69, Protein: 3 gm., Fat: 6 gm., Carbohydrates: 6 gm.*

Makes approx. 2 cups

See photo on front cover.

1 recipe Tofu "Cheese," page 32

1/2 tsp. dried marjoram

1/2 tsp. dried thyme

2 - 3 tsp. lemon juice

2 - 4 cloves garlic, finely minced

1/2 - 3/4 cups unsalted margarine

1/3 cup fresh chervil, minced
   (fresh taragon or dill may be
   substituted --flavor will differ,
   however)

2/3 cup parsley, finely minced

1 - 1 1/2 cups walnuts or pecans,
   lightly toasted and chopped
   (optional for cheese ball only)

# Hot Herb Cheese Puffs

Serves a party of 25

See photo on front cover.

1/2 recipe Tofu Boursin, page 33
1/4" - 1/3" thick slices of whole
   wheat or white bread
several tablespoons margarine
round cookie cutter
   (other shapes can also be used)

*Use the Tofu "Boursin" to make these delicious little canapés. Piping hot from the oven, they're the perfect thing to serve with an aperitif or cocktail. Since they can be assembled in a matter of seconds if you have the "cheese" on hand, you can always surprise your guests with a gourmet treat when they surprise you by showing up unexpectedly.*

Trim the crust off the bread slices and cut into circles with a cookie cutter, preferably 1 1/2" in diameter. Melt the margarine in a skillet and sauté the bread circles on one side until they are just a light, golden brown. These are now called "croûtes." With a teaspoon, pile about 2 tsp. of the cheese onto the uncooked side of the croûtes, pressing lightly with the concave side of the spoon to make smooth little mounds. Place on a cookie sheet and bake in a 375° oven for 8-10 minutes until golden brown. Serve immediately.

*Per serving: Calories: 55, Protein: 2 gm., Fat: 1 gm., Carbohydrates: 7 gm.*

# Tofu "Feta" Cheese

*As close to the real thing as it gets.*

The Tofu "Cheese" for this recipe doesn't need to marinate for a full week if you'd rather use it sooner; about 5 days would do. Break the marinated "Cheese" into 1/2" pieces, place in a container, add the salt and fill with enough olive oil to cover the pieces. Cover and marinate 12 to 24 hours. Drain to use in salads or in pasta recipes. The olive oil can be reused as long as it smells fresh.

*Per 1/4 cup serving: Calories: 314, Protein: 15 gm., Fat: 6 gm., Carbohydrates: 38 gm.*

*Makes 1 cup*

*1 cup Tofu "Cheese,"*
*    page 32*
*olive oil*
*1 - 2 tsp. salt*

# Tofu Cream Cheese Spread with Herbs

*Makes about 1 cup*

8 - 9 oz. well-pressed tofu

3 Tbsp. safflower oil

1 tsp. salt

1 tsp. thyme

1/2 tsp. basil

1/4 tsp. marjoram

2 Tbsp. fresh chives, minced

1/4 cup fresh parsley, minced

2 tsp. lemon juice (optional)

*This is a simple and easy-to-make spread with herbs for bread, crackers, and tasty cucumber sandwiches.*

If you are pressing your own tofu, start with 12 - 14 oz. and follow the directions on page 24. Blend the tofu, oil, salt, and dried herbs in a food processor until perfectly creamy. Fold in the fresh chives and parsley. Add lemon juice for a tangy flavor, if desired. Refrigerate for several hours or overnight to allow flavors to mingle and develop. Keeps for several days.

*Per 2 Tbsp. serving: Calories: 83, Protein: 4 gm., Fat: 7 gm., Carbohydrates: 2 gm.*

# Guacamole Nishimoto

*Makes 1 - 1 1/2 cups*

*People have told me that this is not just guacamole, but great guacamole. Actually, there is hardly anything to making it. I think the secret lies in deleting the lemon juice called for in most recipes.*

Mash the avocado and mix with the remaining ingredients, adding salt and tabasco to taste. I find that the "hotness" decreases as the dish stands, so I always add more at the beginning. Leave the pit in the dip until serving time to prevent discoloration.

Serve with crackers, chips, or use as a spread for bread or canapés.

*Per 1/4 cup serving: Calories: 87, Protein: 1 gm., Fat: 8 gm., Carbohydrates: 5 gm.*

*1 large, ripe avocado*
*1/2 small onion, finely minced*
*1/2 tomato, chopped in little*
*   pieces*
*salt to taste*
*Tabasco sauce to taste*

# Guacamole Vinaigrette Dip

*Makes approx. 1 cup*

*An elegant guacamole. Stuff leaves of Belgian endive or hollowed-out cherry tomatoes with this for an hors d'ouevres platter.*

Mash the avocado and cream with the dressing. Add salt and pepper to taste. If you are not going to use it immediately, leave the pit in the dip to prevent discoloration.

*Per 1/4 cup serving: Calories: 105, Protein: 1 gm., Fat: 10 gm., Carbohydrates: 4 gm.*

*1 large, ripe avocado*
*1/4 - 1/3 cup Basic Vinaigrette,*
*   plain, mustard, garlic or herb*
*   (page 176)*
*freshly ground pepper*
*   and salt  to taste*

# MOUSSES, PÂTÉS, and TERRINES

Here is a selection of some of the most impressive-looking delicacies you will encounter. Garnished properly, they may even look too beautiful to eat. Most are fairly simple to make and require few seasonings, allowing the sweetness and flavor of the vegetables to come through. Although the mousses can be made in a large mold, they will look nicer in individual ones. If you do not own fancy mousse molds, use custard or espresso cups, cupcake tins, or a square baking dish and cut them into small squares. The terrines and pâtés can be made in small bread pans or ring molds, then sliced. The mousses and terrines set with agar can be easily removed from their molds by inserting a thin knife or toothpick between the mousse and the mold, then knocking on the mold lightly.

Most of the baked terrines and pâtés will keep for a week or longer if refrigerated; some even improve in taste if left to sit for a couple of days. The ones made with agar should be eaten within a day or two.

# Carrot and Mushroom Terrine

Serves 8-12

*The sweetness of carrots comes out wonderfully and is counterbalanced by the "meatiness" of this terrine. This can be part of a cold table, sliced and served as is or with a light mustard sauce, or it can be sliced and sautéed for sandwiches.*

In a covered pan sauté the onions and carrots in the oil until relatively soft. Mix with the raw minced mushrooms, walnuts, miso, soy sauce, brandy, and sage. Purée the tofu in a food processor or blender until creamy and combine with the carrot mixture. Add the breadcrumbs last and mix well. Season with salt and pepper to taste, adjusting the seasonings as necessary. Line a loaf pan with brown paper that has been saturated with oil, then fill with this mixture. Fold the oiled paper loosely on top and cover with two sheets of aluminum foil with several holes in the top. Otherwise, pack in a greased terrine mold. Bake at 375° for about 1 1/2 hours, removing the aluminum foil halfway through. Allow to cool before removing from the pan. Let sit overnight to let flavors develop.

*Per serving: Calories: 191, Protein: 8 gm., Fat: 7 gm., Carbohydrates: 23 gm.*

1 onion, minced

1 lb. carrots, grated

1 Tbsp. oil

8 oz. mushrooms, minced

1/2 cup walnuts, ground

2 Tbsp. miso

1 Tbsp. soy sauce

2 Tbsp. brandy or cognac

1 1/2 tsp. sage, dried
   or 2 Tbsp. fresh

12 - 14 oz. tofu, pressed,
   or 8 oz. pre-pressed

1 2/3 cups dry breadcrumbs

salt and pepper to taste

# Green Pea Mousse with Carrot Garnish

*Serves 10-14*

*The Green Pea Mousse:*

*3 cups carrot sticks*

*mild stock or water to cover carrots*

*2 tsp. honey (for the carrots)*

*salt to taste*

*1 onion, chopped*

*1 Tbsp. margarine or oil*

*1 lb. frozen green peas*

*1 1/2 cups water*

*1 Tbsp. honey or maple syrup (for the peas)*

*3 Tbsp. white wine*

*2/3 cup soy milk*

*2 bars, 2 tsp. powdered, or 8 Tbsp. flaked agar*

*1 cup steamed mushrooms or asparagus (optional)*

*This can be very pretty indeed with a bright orange border of delicately seasoned carrots and a brilliant green pea mousse enclosing a row of mushrooms or other vegetable down the middle. It is also easier to make than it looks. It can be served as is or with a dollop of Tofu-Herb Sauce on the side.*

To make this, you will need a narrow bread pan, an oblong or half-moon shaped mold, a ring mold, or individual ramekins or custard cups. You can improvise by cutting one side off a quart-size milk carton and using it as the mold.

First, cook the carrots until tender in enough water or mild stock to cover with the honey and salt. Drain and run under cold water to set the color. Drain again.

Line the container with a layer of the cooked carrot sticks. Lay them down next to each other, being sure to cover every bit of space. This is much easier than it sounds. Cover the entire bottom of the mold and stack or line the carrots carefully to cover the sides as well.

For the Green Pea Mousse, sauté the onion in the margarine or oil in a covered saucepan until tender. Add the green peas, 1 1/2 cups of water, honey, and wine. Cook for 3 to 5 minutes until the peas are just tender but do not overcook as this will greatly affect the color of the mousse. Drain, reserving the liquid. Measure the liquid; you should have about a cup. If you have more, boil it down rapidly to one cup.

Purée the peas in a blender or food processor with the soy milk until completely smooth. Season with salt and pepper. Dissolve the agar in the reserved liquid (see instructions on page 10). Add to the green pea mixture and blend for 15 seconds, then immediately pour it into the carrot-lined mold. Place the steamed mushrooms in a row down the middle, covering the entire length; if you are using steamed asparagus, cover the surface of the mousse with it. Chill for at least four hours, or overnight. At serving time, unmold onto a large plate. Slice and serve with Tofu Herb Sauce.

For the Tofu Herb Sauce, blend all the ingredients except the herbs until very smooth and creamy. Add the finely minced herbs and season to taste with salt and pepper. Chill several hours to allow the flavors to blend and develop.

*Per serving: Calories: 101, Protein: 4 gm., Fat: 2 gm., Carbohydrates: 14 gm.*

*Tofu Herb Sauce:*
*6 oz. tofu*
*    or 3/4 cup, crumbled*
*3 Tbsp. white wine*
*1 tsp. lemon juice*
*1 Tbsp. olive oil*
*1 Tbsp. each fresh chopped chives,*
*    dill and tarragon, or other*
*    herbs of choice*
*salt and pepper to taste*

# Pâté En Croûte

Serves 16

See photo on front cover.

Pâté Crust:

18 oz. whole wheat pastry flour
     (about 4 cups)

1 tsp. salt

1 1/4 cups margarine

2 1/2 Tbsp. tahini dissolved in
     enough ice water to make 3/4
     cup

*This is a pâté that has been baked in a crust and looks splendid on a buffet table—very much like its non-vegetarian counterpart. Seasoned with allspice, cinnamon, garlic, and herbs, and containing ground nuts and whole pistachios, you would never believe that the base was ground gluten. The crust is flaky and tasty the day it is baked, but since the pâté improves in flavor if allowed to sit for a day or two, the crust becomes more of a decoration, although it is perfectly edible. Assembling the pâté is easy if the pastry and gluten have been prepared in advance.*

*Although a large bread pan or two can be used, a traditional pâté mold held together by pins works best and is easier to remove.*

To make the crust, mix the flour and salt in a large bowl. Cut in the margarine with a pastry cutter or processor until it resembles coarse meal. Add the water and tahini mixture and gather it all into a ball. Chill for at least one hour before rolling out.

While the dough is being chilled, make the pâté. Sauté the onion in a tablespoon of the margarine over low heat in a covered pan. Combine the remaining margarine with the rest of the ingredients and season to taste with salt and pepper. Adjust the seasoning if necessary, adding a little more allspice, miso or other spices.

Divide the dough into two balls, reserving about a quarter of the dough for the top crust, plus some extra to cut into little rectangles, squares, circles, and triangles for decorating the pâté crust. Roll out the larger ball on a pastry cloth or lightly floured board to 1/4" thick. The size and shape of your mold or bread pan will determine the size and shape of your dough. Roll it big enough to cover the bottom and allow about an inch beyond the sides. Fit it into the pâté mold or bread pan. Pack in the pâté mixture and fold over the extra dough from the sides. Roll out the top crust and place over the pâté, joining with the sides, and trimming where necessary. Brush the top with a little soy milk or melted margarine and decorate with shapes made with the extra dough. Brush the shapes with soy milk. Make two chimneys in the top of the dough by inserting two pastry tubes or cutting out two 1/2" holes, and prick the top crust all over with a fork. The chimneys and holes allow the stream to escape during baking. Bake in a preheated 350° oven for 1 3/4 hours, covering the top loosely with aluminum foil half-way through to prevent the crust from darkening.

When cool, remove the pastry tubes and take the pâté en croûte out of the mold. Wrap well and allow to sit in the refrigerator for a day or two for best flavor, although it can be served the same day after completely cooling. The spices do take 36-48 hours to develop their full flavor, but the pâté is tasty even with less time. Slice and serve with a fork.

*Per serving: Calories: 488, Protein: 18 gm., Fat: 26 gm., Carbohydrates: 41 gm.*

*Pâté Mixture:*
*1 large onion, minced*
*1/3 cup margarine, melted*
*3 1/2 cups gluten, ground*
  *(page 153)*
*1 1/2 cups nuts, ground*
  *(walnuts, almonds, pecans,*
  *and a few cashews can be used*
  *in combination, or use all*
  *walnuts or pecans)*
*1/3 cup soy milk or cream*
*1 - 1 1/2 cups bread crumbs*
*1/3 - 1/2 cup shelled pistachios*
*1/3 cup brandy or cognac*
*1/2 cup parsley, chopped*
*1/2 tsp. thyme*
*1 tsp. allspice*
*3/4 tsp. cinnamon*
*1/2 tsp. cloves*
*1/4 tsp. nutmeg*
*3 to 4 cloves garlic, minced*
*1 Tbsp. miso*
*salt and pepper to taste*

# Vegetable Aspic Terrine

Serves 6-10

See photo on page 49.

**The Consommé:**

3 1/2 cups good vegetable stock

3 Tbsp. madeira wine

6 - 8 fennel seeds

1/8 tsp. tarragon

1 tsp. tomato paste

salt or soy sauce to taste

3/4 bar, 3/4 tsp. powdered, or 3
  Tbsp. flaked agar

**The Vegetables:**

1/2 onion, quartered and
  separated into leaves

4 sticks asparagus

4 carrot sticks the length of your
  mold or bread pan

1/2 to 1 sweet red pepper, cut into
  strips 1/4" wide

1 cup broccoli florets

1 cup or more small mushrooms

1 pack enoki (white straw)
  mushrooms, optional

*This is absolutely beautiful to look at and very delicately flavored. Seasoned vegetable jewels are held together by a clear jellied consommé which rests on a bedding of bright green pea or asparagus mousse. Impress your boss with this one.*

Combine all the ingredients for the consommé, except the agar, in a large saucepan with a tight-fitting lid. The vegetables will be cooked in this, and both the consommé and vegetables will benefit from the joint simmering. Bring the consommé to a gentle boil and cook the vegetables in it, a few pieces at a time, until they are tender but still crisp. Remove the vegetables as they cook and drain well in a colander placed over a bowl to catch the drippings. Strain and measure the broth. If you have more than 2 cups, boil it down rapidly to two cups. Check the flavor; you might have to adjust the seasonings with a little additional salt, soy sauce, madeira or tomato paste.

Prepare the agar as instructed on page 10 and dissolve it in the 2 cups of consommé. Immediately pour 1/3" into a 1 qt. bread pan or terrine mold and set it over a tray of ice or in the freezer for a few minutes until it begins to jell slightly. Start layering the cooked vegetables, making sure to leave a 1/2" space on both sides or the terrine will crumble when cut. Broccoli flowers look pretty down the middle surounded by carrot sticks and asparagus. Pour a little more hot consommé into the mold, being careful not to disrupt the layer of vegetables inside, and allow it to jell slightly before layering in more vegetables. Repeat this process of layering vegetables, pouring in consommé, and allowing it to partially set until all the consommé is used up (you will probably have some vegetables left over). This takes time as the consommé must thicken slightly before the vegetables can be put in and held in place. Don't allow it to harden completely during the process. A few minutes in the freezer each time more consommé has been poured in is all that is necessary to get it to the proper soft-jell consistency.

You will have plenty of time while the consommé is jelling to make the green pea or asparagus mousse. Cook the peas or asparagus with the onion in the stock with the honey and salt until tender. Drain, reserving the liquid. Purée the vegetables with the soy milk or cream, then dissolve the agar in the remaining stock (you should have at least 1/4 cup or more). Add it to the puréed vegetables and blend for ten seconds. Pour this very carefully on top of the consommé and vegetable mold when it has jelled slightly. Chill several hours or overnight, and carefully invert on to a plate. Slice and serve.

*Per serving: Calories: 51, Protein: 3 gm., Fat: 0 gm., Carbohydrates: 9 gm.*

*The Pea or Asparagus Base:*
*1/2 cup green peas,*
  *fresh or frozen,*
  *or 1 cup asparagus*
*1/4 small onion*
*stock to cover the vegetables*
*1/2 tsp. honey*
*salt to taste*
*1/2 cup soy milk or cream*
*1/2 bar, 1/2 tsp. powdered, or 2*
  *Tbsp. flaked agar*

# Mushroom Mousse with Tarragon-Wine Sauce

*Makes 6-8 small but rich mousses*

*Rich and smooth, a friend thought this tasted like a fine liver mousse. Agar and arrowroot (or kuzu) are used in combination to produce a delicate texture.*

2 Tbsp. oil or margarine

3 Tbsp. shallots, minced

1/2 lb. mushrooms, sliced

3 fresh shiitake mushrooms, sliced

3 Tbsp. white wine

3/4 tsp. tarragon

2 Tbsp. walnuts, chopped

1 1/3 cups rich soy milk or cream

1 Tbsp. kuzu
   or 1 1/2 Tbsp. arrowroot or
   cornstarch

1/2 bar or 1/2 tsp. powdered agar
   (or 2 Tbsp. flakes)

1 recipe Tarragon Wine Sauce,
   page 71

Heat the oil or margarine in a heavy-bottomed saucepan and sauté the shallots until tender. Add the mushrooms and shiitake, cover the pan, and sauté over low heat for a few minutes, letting the mushroom juices exude. Add the wine, cook two or three minutes to get rid of the sharpness, then pour off 1/2 cup of the liquid in the pan into another container. Add the tarragon, walnuts, and soymilk to the pan and continue cooking, covered, for another 10 to 15 minutes. Purée the mixture in a blender or food processor until smooth. Return this to the saucepan.

Dissolve the kuzu or arrowroot in a small amount of water and add it to the purée in the saucepan, stirring while cooking over low heat until the mixture thickens. Prepare the agar according to the directions on page 10, adding it to 1/2 cup of reserved mushroom juices. Mix well. Place this in a small saucepan and turn the heat on high. After it comes to a boil, turn the heat down a bit, and continue cooking for 2 to 3 minutes until the agar is completely dissolved, stirring occasionally. Whisk this into the mushroom mixture and immediately pour into individual molds or dishes. Chill for several hours before unmolding and serving. Serve with chilled Tarragon Wine Sauce, page 71, poured around. Garnish with a sprig of fresh tarragon, if desired.

*Per serving: Calories: 153, Protein: 6 gm., Fat: 9 gm., Carbohydrates: 8 gm.*

# Carrot and Cashew Mousse

*This delicate mousse, slightly sweet from the carrots and cashews, will delight both adults and children, even if they swear they hate carrots. This is best made the day before serving.*

Place the carrots, cashews, onion, stock, and honey in a small covered saucepan. Bring to a boil, then reduce the heat and simmer until the carrots and cashews are very soft. Strain, reserving the stock for later.

Purée the carrot mixture in a blender or food processor with the soy milk and wine. Steam or cook the peas, mushrooms, and ginko nuts in a small amount of water until tender. Season lightly with salt and pepper.

Measure the reserved stock. If you have more than a 1/2 cup left, boil down rapidly over high heat until it has been reduced to 1/2 cup. Prepare the agar as described on page 10, and shred and dissolve in the 1/2 cup of stock, keeping covered while simmering. Add it to the carrot mixture in the blender and blend for twenty to thirty seconds. Mix in the green peas, mushrooms and ginkgo nuts by hand. Immediately pour into molds. Chill overnight in the refrigerator and unmold at serving time. Pour Cashew Crème Sauce around it, if desired.

A note on ginkgo nuts: They are available shelled, cooked, and canned in Oriental food stores. Use them right out of the can without cooking. If only unshelled ones are available, dry-roast them in a pan for 5 or 6 minutes, then crack them to remove the golden nutmeat inside.

*Per serving: Calories: 51, Protein: 2 gm., Fat: 2 gm., Carbohydrates: 7 gm.*

*Makes 6 small mousses*

*2 carrots, sliced 1/4" thick*

*2 Tbsp. raw cashews*

*1/4 medium onion, sliced*

*1 1/4 cups vegetable stock*

*1 tsp. honey*

*1/2 - 1/3 cup rich soy milk or cream*

*1 1/2 Tbsp. white wine*

*3 Tbsp. frozen green peas*

*3 - 4 mushrooms, quartered*

*10 - 12 ginkgo nuts, shelled (optional)*

*salt and white pepper to taste*

*1/2 bar, 1/2 tsp. powdered, or 2 Tbsp. flaked agar*

*1/2 recipe Cashew Crème Sauce, page 80 (optional)*

# Spinach and Basil Mousse

Serves 8-10

*Another wonderful combination that goes perfectly with a little Cashew Mayonnaise, page 80. Make it at the height of summer when fresh basil abounds in either your garden or the supermarket.*

1 medium onion, chopped

1 clove garlic, minced

2 Tbsp. salad oil
   or a good olive oil

1 lb. fresh spinach, washed
   and roughly chopped

8 oz. pressed tofu

1 - 3 Tbsp. lemon juice

grated rind of 1/2 small lemon

8 oz. fresh basil

1/2 cup raw cashews

3/4 cup water

2 Tbsp. white wine

salt and white pepper to taste

1 bar, 1 tsp. powdered,
   or 4 Tbsp. flaked agar

2/3 cup vegetable stock

2 Tbsp. arrowroot
   or 1 Tbsp. kuzu

Sauté the onion and garlic in the oil until soft. Add the spinach and continue cooking until the spinach is fairly tender but still a deep green. Place the spinach mixture, tofu, lemon juice and rind, and the basil in a food processor or blender and blend until very smooth. Remove and pour into a bowl. Rinse out the blender or food processor and purée the cashews and water until creamy and thick. Combine with the spinach-tofu mixture. Add the wine and season with salt and pepper. Pour all of this back into the food processor.

Dissolve the agar in the stock as described on page 10. Before turning off the heat, dissolve the arrowroot or kuzu in a small amount of water and add to the simmering agar, stirring constantly until thickened. Immediately blend into the tofu-spinach-cashew mixture and pour into individual molds or ramekins. Chill completely. After several hours you will be able to unmold these delicate mousses and decorate them prettily with Cashew Mayonnaise, page 80.

*Per serving: Calories: 125, Protein: 6 gm., Fat: 3 gm., Carbohydrates: 8 gm.*

*Vegetable Aspic Terrine, pgs. 44-5*

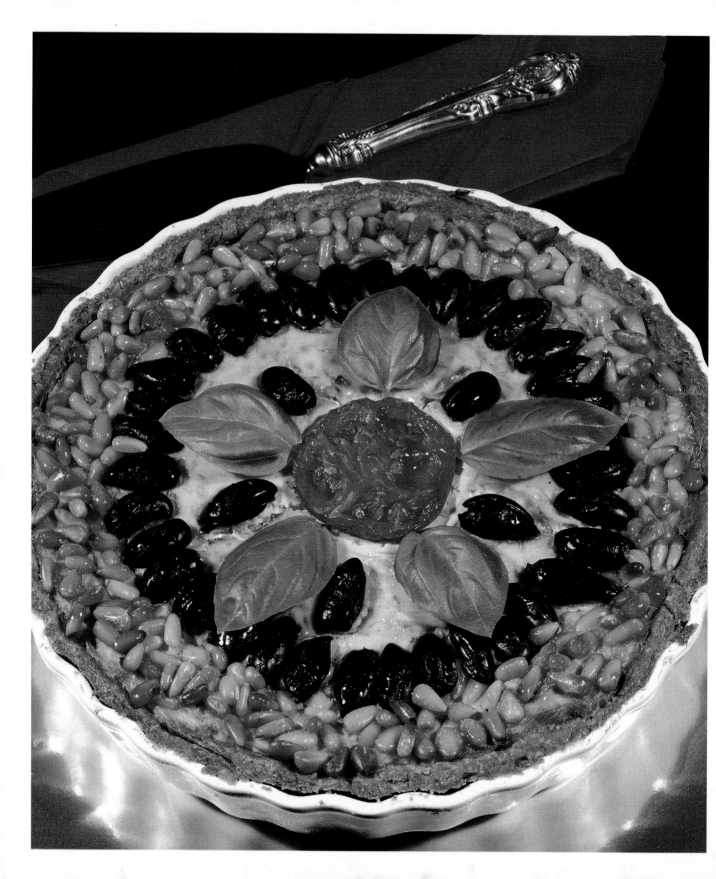

# Eggplant and Tofu Pâté

*Unsuspecting Japanese friends praised me for this "delicious liver pâté" and were surprised when I told them that it contained no meat. This is a soft, spreadable pâté, great on bread and crackers. It is also tasty thinly sliced and sautéed until browned for sandwiches.*

Bake the eggplants whole at 350° until a fork pierces easily through (the length of time will vary with the size of the eggplants). Cut in half and scoop out the pulp, measuring 1 2/3 cups. Discard the skins. Beat the pulp with a fork or beater until creamed.

Sauté the onions in 1 Tbsp. oil until tender. Mix all the ingredients and adjust the seasonings as necessary. The amount of miso will depend on its saltiness; increase or decrease as necessary.

Line a loaf pan with brown paper that has been saturated with oil. If you are using an earthenware terrine mold with a lid, simply oil the mold. Fill with the pâté mixture and fold the oiled brown paper loosely over the top. Cover with a lid that has a steam vent or use a double layer of aluminum foil with several holes in it for steam to escape. Bake in a 350° oven for two hours with a pan of hot water underneath, then remove the water and continue baking for an additional 30 minutes. Do not attempt to remove the pâté from the pan while it is warm. Let cool completely, then refrigerate for 36 to 48 hours before serving. Keeps refrigerated for up to two weeks.

*Per serving: Calories: 140, Protein: 6 gm., Fat: 8 gm., Carbohydrates: 8 gm.*

1 2/3 cups baked eggplant pulp
   (1 very large or two medium
   eggplants)
1 large onion, finely chopped
1 Tbsp. oil, as necessary
1 2/3 cups roasted almond and
   walnuts, mixed and ground
   finely
approximately 1/3 cup mild miso
1/3 cup plus 1 Tbsp. tahini
   or sesame butter
12 oz. tofu , pressed
   (about 8 oz. pre-pressed,
   see page 24)
1 Tbsp. raw ginger, grated
1/2 tsp. allspice
black pepper, freshly ground

*Greek Olive and Basil Quiche, pg. 58*

## SAVORY PASTRIES: TINY TARTS, QUICHES, AND OTHER DELIGHTS:

Although a little extra time and effort are required to make individual tarts and pastries, you will find that they are also a great deal more fun to eat and look at. A silver platter loaded with tasty looking savory tidbits will tempt everyone.

If you are short on time and patience, most of the following can be baked in a large pie pan and cut into slices, but they will lose some of their visual appeal.

Tarts can be filled with a variety of savory items, and aside from the specific recipes in this section, you will find other mixtures throughout the book that could fill a tart or two. Either the Zucchini and Fennel Filling, page 30, or mushrooms or spinach creamed with the White Wine, Soubise, or Béchamel sauces (see pages 62 through 70) would be delicious. Use your imagination to create different combinations of sauces, vegetables, and legumes to fill pastry shells.

Assembling pastries goes rapidly if the pie crust and fillings have been made in advance. Fill and bake them twenty minutes before serving. Most of the crusts and fillings can be made days ahead of time and refrigerated or frozen, so you can even make enough for two occasions and freeze a batch.

Fancy miniature tart shells can be purchased inexpensively at most cookware shops. You can also use muffin tins or custard cups, although they are considerably deeper than tart tins. Although quiches can be baked in a large pan and cut, softer fillings, like creamed mushrooms, do better if baked in individual shells.

Unless specified, the following savory pastries can be made with any of the pie crusts on pages 231-4.

# Smoked Tofu, Mushroom, and Garlic Canapés

*A variable recipe for any number of servings*

*This was a hit at a large party we held. The combination of flavors is superb, and the little treasures are easy to assemble. Expect each person to down several of these.*

Have the tofu marinating from the day before, if possible. It will be cooked just before assembly.

Place the bulbs of garlic in aluminum foil and sprinkle with olive oil. Close up the foil and bake in a moderate oven until tender, about 20 to 30 minutes. Set aside until assembly time.

Prepare croûtes by cutting out bread circles from the thin slices of bread with a 1 1/2" circular cookie cutter. Melt the margarine, corn, or olive oil in a skillet and sauté the bread circles over low heat on one side until golden brown.

Heat the oven to 400°. Rinse and prepare the mushrooms. If large, cut in half; otherwise leave whole. Heat a few tablespoons of oil or margarine in a skillet, and over medium-high heat sauté the mushrooms until tender and browned. Do not cook on low heat or juices will flow out of the mushrooms and they will not brown properly. Season with salt.

While the mushrooms are cooking, sauté the marinated tofu as directed on page 165. When browned, cut into squares the approximate size of the croûtes (bread circles).

Now assemble the canapés. Separate the garlic into cloves and squeeze out the tender meat inside onto the croûtes (one clove per croûte). Spread with a knife. Top with a slice of tofu and garnish with a mushroom.

Place on a cookie sheet and bake for 3 - 4 minutes. Serve while hot.

*Per canapé: Calories: 45, Protein: 2 gm., Fat: 2 gm., Carbohydrates: 3 gm.*

marinated smoked-flavor tofu,
   page 165
1 clove garlic per canapé
several Tbsp. olive oil
thin slices of whole wheat
   or white bread (a closely
   textured bread works best)
margarine, corn, or olive oil
one mushroom per canapé
   if very small,
   or 1/2 per canapé if large

# Curried Mushroom Tarts

*Serves anywhere from 6-16 depending on the size of the tarts*

dough for 1 whole wheat pie crust
   of your choice
    (see pages 231-4)
2 Tbsp. shallots or green onions,
   minced
8 oz. mushrooms, sliced
4 oz. fresh or reconstituted
   shiitake mushrooms, sliced
2 Tbsp. oil or margarine
2 Tbsp. flour
3 Tbsp. madeira wine
1 1/4 cups rich soy milk or cream,
1/4 to 1/2 tsp. curry powder
salt and pepper to taste

*A rich, creamy mushroom filling seasoned lightly with curry. An especially quick recipe to prepare.*

Prepare the pie crust and roll out 1/8" thick. Line small tart shells or muffin tins. Prick the bottoms all over with a fork. Chill until later.

Sauté the shallots, mushrooms, and shiitake mushrooms in the oil or margarine over medium heat until tender. Turn down the heat to low and add the flour. Cook two minutes, stirring constantly. Add the madeira, cook a moment, then add the soy milk or cream, stirring constantly. Cook gently over low heat until thickened, again stirring continuously. Flavor with curry powder, starting with 1/4 teaspoon. Keep the curry flavor light. Season with salt, pepper and perhaps a touch more of madeira. Fill the prepared shells and bake for fifteen minutes in a preheated 400° oven. Serve immediately.

For *Mushroom and Tarragon Tarts*, follow the above recipe but delete the curry powder and add a 1/2 teaspoon of dried tarragon. If possible, substitute oyster mushrooms for the shiitake. A deliciously distinctive recipe.

*Per medium tart: Calories: 161, Protein: 4 gm., Fat: 10 gm., Carbohydrates: 15*

# Provençale Spinach Tarts

*Another very tasty and quick recipe.*

Line tart shells with pie crust rolled out 1/8" thick. Prick all over with a fork. Pre-bake for 3 - 4 minutes at 400°.

Sauté the onions and garlic in the olive oil, then add the spinach and cook until soft and most of the water has evaporated. Add the chopped tomato and cook another 3 or 4 minutes. Season with salt and pepper. Add the toasted pine nuts, fill the pre-baked tart shells, and top with soy cheese, if desired. Bake for 10 minutes at 375°. Serve immediately.

*Per medium tart: Calories: 174, Protein: 3 gm., Fat: 9 gm., Carbohydrates: 15 gm.*

*Serves anywhere from 6-16*

*dough for 1 whole wheat pie crust
   of your choice
   (see pages 231-4)*
*1 onion, minced*
*2 - 3 cloves garlic, minced*
*3 Tbsp. olive oil*
*1 small bunch spinach,
   thoroughly washed, dried, and
   roughly chopped*
*1 ripe but firm tomato, finely
   chopped*
*salt and pepper to taste*
*1/4 cup pine nuts, lightly toasted*
*1/2 cup soy cheese, grated
   (optional)*

# Spinach Napoleons

*Makes 32 pieces.*

*See photo on front cover.*

1 medium onion, chopped fine

3 - 8 Tbsp. melted margarine or
    olive oil

1 bunch spinach

1 bunch dill, chopped

8 oz. tofu, firm or pressed (see
    page 24)

2 Tbsp. margarine

4 Tbsp. flour

1 cup hot soy milk

1/4 tsp. nutmeg

salt and pepper to taste

8 leaves filo

*Puff pastry may be substituted for the filo leaves.*

Sauté the onion in 1 Tbsp. of the melted margarine or olive oil until tender. Clean and chop the spinach, add to the onion, and sauté until wilted. Keep sautéing until most of the juices have evaporated. Add the chopped dill and sauté another 2 - 3 minutes. Season with salt and pepper to taste. Crumble the tofu and dry fry over very low heat for 10 - 15 minutes stirring constantly until it resembles dry curds.

Make a thick white sauce by melting the 2 Tbsp. margarine in a small sauce pan and whisking in the flour. Add the hot soy milk all at once, stirring constantly, and cook for 2 - 3 minutes. Season with the nutmeg, and salt and pepper to taste. Combine the sauce with the tofu.

Oil an 8" square pan. Rapidly put 1 filo leaf down in the pan, brush with the melted margarine or olive oil, and fold the overhanging edges of the leaf back in over itself. Lay down another leaf and repeat the process using a total of four leaves. Spread the tofu mixture evenly over the leaves and then spread the spinach mixture down over the tofu. Repeat the brushing and folding process with the other four leaves of filo. Bake at 350° for 25 - 30 minutes until nicely brown. Cut into 1" by 2" squares and serve.

*Per piece: Calories: 50, Protein: 2 gm., Fat: 4 gm., Carbohydrates: 3 gm.*

# Basic Quiche

*Here is a basic tofu quiche recipe with several variations. Although they contain no eggs, cream, milk, or cheese, I think they are every bit as delicious as their dairy counterparts. A little turmeric will add the golden egg color.*

Cream the tofu, soy milk, oil, and turmeric in a blender or food processor until absolutely smooth. Sauté the onion in oil until soft, then combine with the tofu mixture in a bowl. Season with salt, pepper, and nutmeg. At this point, add various ingredients as suggested in the variations below, or use as is to fill shells.

Roll out the crust 1/8" thick and line a 9" pie pan or individual tart shells. Pre-bake the shells in a 400° oven, 3 - 4 minutes for small tartlets, 10 - 12 minutes for a 9" pan. Fill with the above mixture and bake in a 350° oven (15 minutes for individual shells or 45 minutes for a large quiche) until the top is firm and puffed up. Serve "quichettes" immediately, but wait 15 minutes before cutting a large quiche. These may also be served at room temperature.

*Per serving: Calories: 123, Protein: 5 gm., Fat: 8 gm., Carbohydrates: 9 gm.*

*Serves 8 - 16 as an appetizer or hors d'ouevres*

*14 - 16 oz. tofu*

*1/2 cup soy milk or cream*

*2 Tbsp. oil (corn oil will give a more buttery flavor)*

*1/4 - 1/2 tsp. turmeric*

*2 medium onions, minced*

*enough oil or margarine for sautéing*

*salt and pepper to taste*

*1/4 - 1/2 tsp. nutmeg, freshly grated if possible*

*dough for 1 whole wheat pie crust of your choice (see pages 231-4)*

# Greek Olive and Basil Quiche

Serves 8 - 16 as an appetizer
or hors d'ouevres

See photo on page 50.

1 recipe Basic Quiche, page 56
fresh basil leaves
pitted Kalamata or oil-cured
  olives, halved
pine nuts (opt.)
1/2 cherry tomato (opt.)

This one is a real winner. You must, however, use excellent oil-cured or Kalamata olives from Greece or Italy. Watery canned American olives just will not do.

Make the basic quiche recipe and fill as directed above. Top each quiche with fresh basil leaves and pitted oil-cured or Kalamata olive halves. Be decorative and throw on some pine nuts, if desired. A cherry tomato cut in half will also add a nice touch. Bake as for the basic quiche recipe.

Per serving: Calories: 138, Protein: 5 gm., Fat: 8 gm., Carbohydrates: 9 gm.

# Curried Carrot Quiche

Serves 8 - 16 as an appetizer
or hors d'ouevres

Cook the carrots and cashews in enough stock to cover. Purée when cool with the curry powder and wine, and add to the Basic Quiche recipe. Top with almond slices and bake as directed in Quiche recipe. Leeks can be substituted for onions.

*Per serving: Calories: 133, Protein: 5 gm., Fat: 8 gm., Carbohydrates: 11 gm.*

3 medium carrots
4 Tbsp. raw cashews
stock for cooking carrots
1 tsp. curry powder
2 Tbsp. white wine
1 recipe Basic Quiche, page 56
almond slices

# Spinach and Dill Quiche

Serves 8 - 16 as an appetizer
or hors d'ouevres

Add the dill and spinach to the Basic Quiche recipe. Fill shells and top with pine nuts or sliced mushrooms. Bake as directed in the Quiche recipe.

*Per serving: Calories: 129, Protein: 5 gm., Fat: 8 gm., Carbohydrates: 10 gm.*

1 recipe Basic Quiche, page 56
3 Tbsp. fresh dill, chopped
1 bunch spinach, steamed,
    drained well, and chopped,
    or 10 oz. frozen, chopped
    spinach, well drained
pine nuts or sliced mushrooms
    (opt.)

# *Mushroom Quiche*

*Serves 8 - 16 as an appetizer
or hors d'oeuvres*

*1 recipe Basic Quiche, page 56*

*1 lb. mushrooms, sliced,
 or a mixture of mushrooms*

*2 - 3 Tbsp. madeira wine
 or sherry (optional)*

*This can be made very interesting by the addition of several types of mushrooms: champignons (the type most often found in your grocery store), shiitake, oyster, or any variety of mild mushroom now available in produce sections. Much of the flavor will come from the champignons, so they should make up half the blend.*

Add the mushrooms to the onions in the basic recipe once the onions are soft and continue sautéing until mushrooms are also soft. Add madeira or sherry, if desired and cook 3-4 minutes to burn off the alcohol. Add to basic recipe and bake as directed.

*Per serving: Calories: 133, Protein: 5 gm., Fat: 8 gm., Carbohydrates: 10 gm.*

# Sauces to Pour On,
# and On and On....

Sauces can do wonders. Yesterday's leftovers will come alive enrobed in a nice sauce, and even a simple vegetable or a few potatoes will somehow seem more worthy of reverence. Licking up every last drop of Madeira Mushroom or Rich Brown Sauce, your guests will ask you where in France you were trained as a chef.

Sauces are thickened in a variety of ways. Traditional white sauces are thickened with a roux (flour and butter), while fancier ones are often made by the reduction method (cooking down) which results in a richer and deeper flavor. Some require a long simmering, while others can be made in just minutes. You will find all sorts of sauces here and learn that even the more complicated-looking ones become easy once the method for making them is acquired.

Many of these freeze nicely, so go ahead and make a large batch. Then when you have some dish that doesn't pack enough punch by itself, you can take out one of your sauces from the freezer to reheat and pour on.

# Béchamel or White Sauce

*Makes about 2 cups*

3 Tbsp. margarine

4 Tbsp. flour (unbleached white
    or whole wheat pastry flour
    with the bran sifted out)

2 cups hot soy or almond milk

1/4 medium onion, separated into
    leaves

4 cloves

6 - 8 peppercorns or white pepper
    to taste

several dashes freshly grated
    nutmeg

1 tsp. maple syrup, if you are
    using an unblended soy milk
    (see page 19)

salt to taste

*This is your traditional white sauce made with soy or almond milk instead of dairy milk. The trick to producing a smooth sauce without lumps is to heat the milk before adding it to the roux (flour and butter). Then it all blends very smoothly with just a few turns of the whisk. And yes, soy milk makes perfectly good béchamel with no "beany" taste if a few tricks are observed. Your guests will never know the difference. For a sauce with more character, try the Soubise Sauce on page 66 or one of the following variations.*

Melt the margarine in a heavy-bottomed pan or the top of a double boiler. Add the flour, and cook for 2 or 3 minutes over low heat. Add the hot milk, stirring with a whisk. It will thicken quickly. Add the onion, cloves, peppercorns, nutmeg, maple syrup, if necessary, and salt to taste. Continue to cook, covered, for 10 to 15 minutes. Stir frequently with a wooden spoon to prevent it from scorching. Strain through a sieve. Use immediately or pour a coating of milk on top to prevent a skin from forming—mix the milk in when you reheat the sauce.

*Quick White Sauce*: Follow the recipe above, but delete the onion, cloves, and peppercorns. Cook only until thickened. Season with salt, pepper, and nutmeg.

*Paprika Sauce*: Add a tablespoon of a good Hungarian paprika to the Béchamel Sauce, whisking until smooth.

*Per 1/4 cup serving: Calories: 75, Protein: 3 gm., Fat: 5 gm., Carbohydrates: 5 gm.*

# Nutty Almond Sauce

*Ground roasted almonds are added to the basic Béchamel Sauce to make a rich and flavorful sauce that is excellent over grains, vegetables, and Wild Rice Crêpes (page 114), as well as in casseroles and gratins.*

Follow the recipe for the Béchamel Sauce (page 62), but allow the margarine to brown a little first (don't let it burn) before adding the flour. Roast a half cup of almonds to a golden brown, then pulverize them in a blender or nut grinder. Add the almonds to the sauce and cook for 4 or 5 minutes. A teaspoon of soy sauce may be added if desired. If you prefer a smoother sauce, you can purée it all, but I like it best with a very fine crunch.

*Per 1/4 cup serving: Calories: 106, Protein: 4 gm., Fat: 5 gm., Carbohydrates: 5 gm.*

*Makes about 2 1/2 cups*

3 Tbsp. margarine

4 Tbsp. flour (unbleached white or whole wheat pastry flour with the bran sifted out)

2 1/2 cups hot soy or almond milk

1/2 cup almonds

1/4 medium onion, separated into leaves

4 cloves

6 - 8 peppercorns or white pepper to taste

several dashes freshly grated nutmeg

1 tsp. maple syrup, if you are using an unblended soy milk (see page 19)

1 tsp. soy sauce (optional)

salt to taste

# Quick Mushroom Sauce

*Makes about 2 1/4 cups*

*1 recipe Béchamel or White*
*Sauce, page 62*
*1/3 - 1/2 lb. mushrooms*
*1 - 2 Tbsp. sherry or white wine*
*(optional)*

Make the basic Béchamel Sauce. While it is simmering, sauté the mushrooms in a separate pan. After straining the sauce, add the mushrooms and cook for another 5 or 6 minutes. A tablespoon or two of sherry or white wine can be added along with the mushrooms, if desired.

*Per 1/4 cup serving: Calories: 71, Protein: 3 gm., Fat: 5 gm., Carbohydrates: 5 gm.*

# Tofu "Mornay" Sauce

*Tofu "Cheese" adds a subtle, cheesy flavor to white sauce.*

Make the Béchamel Sauce, and after straining, whisk in the crumbled "cheese." Reheat and serve.

*Per 1/4 cup serving: Calories: 104, Protein: 4 gm., Fat: 5 gm., Carbohydrates: 9 gm.*

*Makes about 2 1/4 cups*

*1 recipe Béchamel Sauce, page 62*
*1/3 to 1/2 cup Tofu "Cheese", page 32*

# Soubise Sauce

*Makes 3 cups*

1 1/4 lb. onions, sliced

4 Tbsp. oil or margarine

1 tsp. salt

4 Tbsp. flour (unbleached white
  or whole wheat pastry flour
  with the bran sifted out

2 1/2 to 3 cups hot soy milk

salt, white pepper, and nutmeg to
  taste

*A traditional Béchamel with the addition of onions. Good in casseroles,
gratins, with pasta or crêpes or brown rice.*

In a covered pan sauté the onions in the oil or margarine
with a teaspoon of salt for 30 to 40 minutes over low heat,
stirring occasionally. Do not let them brown. Add the flour
and cook for one minute, stirring constantly. Add the hot
soy milk and whisk continuously until smooth and thick.
Partially cover and continue cooking for another 15 minutes
over low heat, stirring occasionally. Be careful not to scorch
the sauce. Purée in a blender or food processor and season
with nutmeg, pepper, and more salt if necessary.

*Per 1/4 cup serving: Calories: 87, Protein: 3 gm., Fat: 6 gm., Carbohydrates: 7
gm.*

# Soubise Sauce Suprême

*Wine and stock are used to replace part of the soy milk to make it lighter and yet give it more character. Use as you would the Soubise Sauce on page 66.*

Sauté the onions with a teaspoon of salt in the margarine in a covered saucepan for 20 minutes until very soft. Add the flour, cook a minute, then add the hot stock and wine, stirring constantly. Simmer gently for 10 minutes, then add the soy milk and continue simmering for 20 more minutes. Purée, diluting with more soy milk if it seems too thick. Season with salt, pepper, and nutmeg to taste.

*Per 1/4 cup serving: Calories: 65, Protein: 2 gm., Fat: 3 gm.,Carbohydrates: 9 gm.*

*Makes 4 1/2 cups*

1 3/4 lbs. onions, sliced

1 tsp. salt

4 Tbsp. margarine

5 Tbsp. flour

1 cup hot, well-flavored stock

1 cup dry white wine

2 to 2 1/2 cups hot soy milk

salt, pepper, and nutmeg to taste

# Tangy White Wine Sauce

*Makes under 2 cups*

*A slightly tangy sauce that is wonderful over crêpes, surrounding bouchées filled with creamed mushrooms, over asparagus, delicately flavored warm terrines, and other elegant concoctions. This is not your typical white sauce that can be cooked up in ten minutes; it takes over an hour of simmering but there is little work involved and the results are fabulous. For those who prefer a slightly sweeter sauce, try the Sweet White Wine Sauce on page 69.*

1 medium onion, sliced

a handful of mushrooms
   or mushroom stems, sliced

1/2 stalk celery, sliced

1 bay leaf

1/4 tsp. thyme

several sprigs parsley

1 cup well-flavored stock

2 3/4 cups dry white wine

10 peppercorns

salt to taste

1 cup soy cream or almond milk

1 tsp. arrowroot to thicken
   (optional)

Place all the ingredients except the soy cream or cashew milk and arrowroot in a covered pot and simmer for one hour or more until it is reduced to 1/4 or less of its original volume. Add the soy or almond milk and simmer gently for 5 minutes. Strain, pressing the juices out of the vegetables. This makes less than 2 cups of sauce, but the recipe can easily be doubled. It is also a much thinner sauce than Béchamel, but a little arrowroot dissolved in water can be added at the end if you prefer it a little thicker.

*Per 1/4 cup serving: Calories: 61,  Protein: 3 gm., Fat: 1 gm., Carbohydrates: 17 gm.*

# Sweet White Wine Sauce

*Slightly sweeter than the preceding recipe.*

Make as for the Tangy White Wine Sauce on page 68. Cashew milk can be used in place of almond milk since it adds a sweetness of its own. Once again, this can be thickened at the end with a little arrowroot, if desired.

*Per 1/4 cup serving: Calories: 38, Protein: 2 gm., Fat: 1 gm., Carbohydrates: 11 gm.*

*Makes under 2 cups*

*1 medium onion, sliced*

*a handful of mushrooms
    or mushroom stems, sliced*

*1/2 stalk celery, sliced*

*1 apple, chopped*

*1 bay leaf*

*1/4 tsp. thyme*

*several sprigs parsley*

*2 3/4 cups well-flavored stock*

*1 cup dry white wine*

*10 peppercorns*

*salt to taste*

*1 cup soy cream, almond milk,
    or cashew milk*

*1 tsp. arrowroot to thicken
    (optional)*

# Instant White Wine Sauce

Makes 1 1/2 cups

1/4 cup onions, minced

2 Tbsp. margarine

2 Tbsp. flour

1/2 cup dry white wine

1 cup hot soy or almond milk

salt, pepper, and nutmeg to taste

*The preceding two white wine sauces are more full flavored, but this one will serve you well if you're short on time.*

Sauté the onions in the margarine until tender. Add the flour and cook for one minute. Add the wine while stirring with a whisk, and cook slowly for 5 or 6 minutes. Add the soy or almond milk, whisking all the while, until smooth and thick. Season to taste with salt, pepper, and nutmeg, and simmer for an additional 5 minutes. If you prefer an absolutely smooth sauce, the onions may be strained out.

*Per 1/4 cup serving: Calories: 71, Protein: 2 gm., Fat: 5 gm., Carbohydrates: 6 gm.*

# Tarragon Wine Sauce

*Serve this with the Mushroom Mousse or a cold terrine or vegetable.*

Add the tarragon to the wine and boil down rapidly until it has been reduced to 6 tablespoons. Add the stock and boil down again to less than 2/3 cup. It is very important that the wine be fully reduced and then boiled and reduced again with the stock, or the soy milk will curdle and sauce will be too tangy. Turn down the heat to low and add the soy milk or cream. Cook gently to allow flavors to mingle, but do not allow it to boil. Season to taste.

Chill completely before serving with Mushroom Mousse (page 46) or cooked, chilled vegetables.

*Per 1/4 cup serving: Calories: 42, Protein: 3 gm., Fat: 1 gm., Carbohydrates: 9 gm.*

*Makes about 1 1/4 cups*

2 tsp. dried tarragon
1 cup dry white wine
1 cup well-flavored stock
1/2 to 1 cup rich soy milk or cream
salt and white pepper to taste

# Teriyaki Sauce and Marinade

Makes 1 1/3 cups


scant 2/3 cup soy sauce

1/3 cup mirin

1/3 cup water

4 - 5 Tbsp. honey

4 Tbsp. hulled sesame seeds

1 tsp. dark Oriental sesame oil

*Dip steamed vegetables in this, or marinate tofu, tempeh, or vegetables before grilling or sautéing.*

Combine the soy sauce, mirin, water, and honey in a small saucepan and bring to a gentle boil. Simmer for one minute. Place the sesame seeds in a small skillet and dry-roast until they give off a nutty aroma and crackle slightly. DO NOT BURN OR ALLOW TO DARKEN. Add to the sauce along with the sesame oil.

Only a small amount of this sauce is needed for dipping. You may dilute it with more water if you want to pour it over vegetables or rice.

*Per 1 Tbsp. serving: Calories: 40, Protein: 1 gm., Fat: 0.5 gm., Carbohydrates: 8 gm.*

# Madeira Mushroom Sauce

*Utterly, incredibly delicious—the kind of sauce that makes life seem worth living! The secret is using stock from stewing gluten (see below). Using anything else will give a less than out-of-this-world result. This is the perfect sauce for crêpes and other wonderful things.*

For the hot gluten stock, follow the directions for making Stove-Top Gluten on page 155 and use onions, celery, and 12-15 dried shiitake, with salt being the only seasoning (no soy sauce, tomatoes, etc.). Drain off the resulting stock and set aside.

Slice the mushrooms and shiitake, and separate the shimeji or oyster mushrooms into individual mushrooms or small clumps. Sauté all the mushrooms in the margarine in a covered saucepan for ten minutes. Add the flour and cook for 2 minutes, stirring constantly. While whisking, add the hot gluten stock and madeira, and cook until slightly thickened. Cover and simmer over low heat for 20 minutes. Uncover, turn heat to high, and boil rapidly to reduce by one-third, stirring occasionally. Season with salt and pepper, adding more madeira, if necessary, for flavor.

*Per 1/4 cup serving: Calories: 55, Protein: 1 gm., Fat: 3 gm., Carbohydrates: 4 gm.*

*Makes about 3-4 cups*

*3 cups hot gluten stock from making gluten (see recipe on page 155)*

*1 lb. mushrooms (use 1/2 lb. brown mushrooms, if available)*

*4 oz. fresh or reconstituted shiitake mushrooms*

*4 oz. fresh shimeji or oyster mushrooms*

*4 Tbsp. margarine*

*1/3 cup onions or shallots, finely minced*

*3 Tbsp. flour (unbleached white or whole wheat pastry flour with the bran sifted out)*

*1/3 to 1/2 cup madeira, or more to taste*

*salt and pepper to taste*

# Rich Brown Sauce

*Makes about 3 cups*

*Friends have often compared this to a demi-glace sauce as they lick every drop off their plates. This is definitely not anything like the lumpy, brown, floury substance called "gravy"; it is rich, with complex over- and undertones. It is excellent with French Moussaka, pages 130-1, Wild Rice Crêpes, page 144, and tofu or tempeh burgers. Any leftover brown sauce can be added to stir-fry vegetables with a little soy sauce for a rich, Oriental flavor. It also freezes beautifully, so make twice the amount and freeze half for later.*

1 1/2 to 2 cups onions, finely
   diced

1 cup celery, diced

1 cup carrots, diced

1 Tbsp. oil or margarine

3 very ripe tomatoes, chopped

1 cup or more red wine

1/2 bulb garlic, sliced
   (half a bulb, not a clove)

6 dried shiitake mushrooms

1/2 cup mushrooms, sliced

2 Tbsp. soy sauce

1 to 2 Tbsp. miso
   (mild or medium)

1/2 tsp. rosemary

1/2 tsp. thyme

3 1/2 to 4 cups good stock

4 Tbsp. margarine

6 Tbsp. flour

In a large covered pot sauté the onions, celery, and carrots in the oil or margarine until relatively tender. Add the tomatoes, wine, garlic, shiitake, mushrooms, soy sauce, miso, and herbs, and bring to a boil. Add the stock. When it has reached a second boil, cover, lower the heat, and simmer for one hour or longer. Taste and adjust seasonings, adding more stock or water if the flavor seems too strong, or boiling down rapidly to concentrate if the flavor seems weak. Set a colander over a bowl and pour it through to strain the vegetables. Press as much juice out of the vegetables as possible and then discard them.

Melt the other 4 tablespoons of margarine and add the flour. Cook for 2 minutes, stirring with a wooden spoon. While whisking, add the hot stock and cook over low heat until thickened.

*Per 1/4 cup serving: Calories: 95, Protein: 2 gm., Fat: 5 gm., Carbohydrates: 12 gm.*

# Brown Sauce Suprême

*An extra portion of vegetables and cooking time results in a superior sauce.*

This sauce is made like the Rich Brown Sauce on page 74, but it will not be thickened with a roux at the end. Prepare the vegetables, seasonings, and stock, and then strain. Sauté the additional 1/2 cups of onions, carrots, and celery until tender, then add the flour to make a roux. Add the hot, strained stock while stirring constantly, then lower the heat, cover, and simmer for an additional 1 to 1 1/2 hours. Strain out the added vegetables. The whole process will involved 2 1/2 to 3 hours of simmering, but the results are grand.

*Per 1/4 cup serving: Calories: 94, Protein: 3 gm., Fat: 2 gm., Carbohydrates: 14 gm.*

*Makes about 4 cups*

3 - 4 cups onions, finely diced

2 cups celery, diced

2 cups carrots, diced

2 Tbsp. oil or margarine

6 very ripe tomatoes, chopped

2 cups or more red wine

1 bulb garlic, sliced
   (one bulb, not one clove)

12 dried shiitake mushrooms

1 cup mushrooms, sliced

1/4 cup soy sauce

2 - 4 Tbsp. miso
   (mild or medium)

1 tsp. rosemary

1 tsp. thyme

7 to 8 cups good stock

1/2 cup onion, finely diced

1/2 cup carrots, diced

1/2 cup celery. diced

6 Tbsp. flour

# Quick Brown Sauce

Makes about 2 1/2 cups.

1 medium onion, minced

1 clove garlic, minced

3 Tbsp. oil or margarine

3 Tbsp. flour

2 cups hot stock

1 cup tomato juice

1/4 cup soy sauce

1 - 2 Tbsp. mild miso

2 Tbsp. mirin

1 Tbsp. red wine vinegar


1/4 cup or more madeira

*A time-saving brown sauce that is fine for many home-style dishes.*

Sauté the onions and garlic in the oil or margarine until soft. Add the flour, cook a minute or two, then add the hot stock, stirring constantly. Add all the remaining ingredients except the madeira and cook rapidly over high heat to reduce by 1/3 to 1/2. Add the madeira, cook a few more minutes, and if desired, add a swirl of margarine in the end to enrich.

*Per 1/4 cup serving: Calories: 76, Protein: 1 gm., Fat: 4 gm., Carbohydrates: 8 gm.*

# Easy Mushroom Brown Sauce

*Here is a tasty sauce that can be whipped up in ten minutes, although you will have to soak the shiitake an hour or so beforehand. This is thickened with arrowroot or kuzu rather than flour, and has a glazed appearance. Serve it over Tofu Burgers (page 118), grains, or vegetables.*

Soak the shiitake in the warm water for about an hour. If you are pressed for time, soak in boiling water for twenty to thirty minutes. Remove, squeeze lightly, and slice thinly. Melt the oil or margarine in a small covered saucepan and saute the mushrooms and shiitake for 4 to 5 minutes until they are partly reduced in size and have begun to exude their juices. Add the sherry or sake, turn the heat up high, and add the garlic, shiitake stock and tomato juice. Boil rapidly for a minute, then add the soy sauce and mirin, and continue boiling for another 2 to 3 minutes. Turn the heat down low and add the nutritional yeast and miso. While stirring constantly, add the arrowroot and cook the sauce until it has thickened and become transparent.

*Per 1/4 cup serving: Calories: 58, Protein: 1 gm., Fat: 4 gm., Carbohydrates: 5 gm.*

*Makes about 2 cups*

4 - 5 dried shiitake mushrooms

1 cup warm water

2 Tbsp. oil or margarine

4 oz. mushrooms, sliced

2 Tbsp. sherry, sake, or wine

1 clove garlic, minced

1/2 cup tomato juice

1 Tbsp. soy sauce

1 Tbsp. mirin

1 - 3 tsp. nutritional yeast

1/2 Tbsp. miso

1 1/2 Tbsp. arrowroot
   or 2 tsp. kuzu dissolved in a
   small amount of water

# Fresh Tomato Sauce

*Makes 2 1/2 - 3 cups*

*Unlike the puréed and long-stewed counterpart, this tomato sauce is made from fresh tomatoes and cooks up in less than a half hour to produce a light, fresh taste. The addition of mushrooms is optional, but they do provide a nice contrast in texture. Serve with vermicelli, linguini, tortellini, or crêpes.*

1 large onion, finely chopped

2 cloves garlic, minced

2 Tbsp. olive oil

2 lbs. fresh, ripe tomatoes,
  chopped (approx. 3 very large
  or 5 - 6 regular)

4 Tbsp. red wine

1 tsp. dried or 3 Tbsp. chopped
  fresh basil

1/2 tsp. rosemary

salt and pepper to taste


1/2 lb. mushrooms, sliced
  (optional)

1 Tbsp. olive oil (optional)

salt to taste (optional)

In a large, covered skillet sauté the onion and garlic in the olive oil until soft. Add the tomatoes and red wine, cover, and cook for 5 minutes. Add the basil and rosemary, cover again, and continue cooking for 20 minutes, stirring occasionally. Season with salt and pepper to taste.

If you want to add mushrooms, sauté them in the olive oil over high heat until lightly browned. Lightly salt and add the sauce and simmer an additional five minutes.

*Per 1/4 cup serving: Calories: 47, Protein: 1 gm., Fat: 3 gm., Carbohydrates: 4 gm.*

# Mushroom Aurora Sauce

*My mother likes this mild tasting but creamy, tasty sauce over her tofu burgers. It is also good over fettucine and crêpes.*

Slice the mushrooms and shiitake thickly and separate the oyster mushrooms into small clumps. Sauté the onions and garlic in the margarine in a covered saucepan until tender, then add the mushrooms. Cover and cook for 5 minutes to release their juices. Add the flour, cook for 2 minutes while stirring, then add the stock and wine, stirring constantly. Simmer gently for a minute. Add the tomatoes, bay leaf, basil, salt, and pepper to taste. Cover and simmer 30 to 40 minutes until the tomatoes have broken down and the sauce has been reduced by at least 1/3. Add the soy milk and gently simmer for another minute.

*Per 1/4 cup serving: Calories: 85, Protein: 2 gm., Fat: 5 gm., Carbohydrates: 7 gm.*

*Makes about 2 1/2 cups*

4 oz. each button, oyster, and
  shiitake mushrooms,
  or 12 oz. mushrooms
1/2 medium onion, minced
2 cloves garlic, minced
4 Tbsp. margarine
5 Tbsp. flour
1 cup hot vegetable stock
  (or the soaking water from
  reconstituting the shiitake if
  dried ones are used)
1/2 cup white wine
2 ripe tomatoes, chopped
1 bay leaf
1/2 tsp. basil
salt and pepper to taste

1/2 cup soy milk or cream

# Cashew Mayonnaise and Crème Sauce

*Makes about 1 cup*

1/2 cup raw cashews

3 Tbsp. lemon juice

1/4 cup water

1/2 cup safflower oil

pinch of salt

*Cashews turn into a lovely, tangy mayonnaise that can accompany vegetable mousses, cold asparagus, canapes, and salads. Diluted with a bit of water, it works as a creamy sauce to surround some of the cold mousses on pages 39-48.*

Place the cashews, lemon juice, and water in the blender and whip until very creamy. Add the oil a little at a time, scraping down the sides whenever necessary, until it becomes very thick and creamy like mayonnaise. Add the salt, blend a moment longer, and refrigerate until needed.

*Cashew Crème Sauce:* Dilute half the Cashew Mayonnaise with an equal amount of water, adding a little at a time, to reach a heavy cream consistency. Add an extra pinch of salt or lemon juice to taste. For a thicker sauce add less water.

*Per 1 Tbsp. serving: Calories: 87, Protein: 1 gm., Fat: 9 gm., Carbohydrates: 2 gm.*

# Dijon Mustard Sauce

*An excellent cold sauce for cold artichokes, asparagus, avocado, and broccoli. Only a small amount is needed.*

In a small bowl beat the boiling water into the mustard a little at a time. Then beat in the olive oil drop by drop so that the entire mixture emulsifies and becomes a thick sauce. Add lemon juice, a half teaspoon at a time, to taste, and season with salt and pepper.

*Per 1 Tbsp. serving: Calories: 80, Protein: 0 gm., Fat: 9 gm., Carbohydrates: 0 gm.*

*Makes 1/2 - 3/4 cup*

*3 Tbsp. boiling water*

*3 Tbsp. Dijon-style mustard*

*1/3 to 1/2 cup good olive oil
(preferably extra virgin)*

*lemon juice, salt, and pepper to
taste*

# Tofu Aïoli

*Serves 4-8*

1/2 - 1 recipe Tofu "Cheese,"
  page 32
2 to 6 cloves garlic, minced or
  pressed
3 - 6 oz. good olive oil
  (extra virgin, if possible)

*Here's a rich, assertive sauce for garlic lovers only. Serve as a dipping sauce for steamed vegetables, potatoes, and cubes of french bread. A bold red wine can accompany this.*

Place the garlic and "Tofu Cheese" in a blender and whiz until smooth, adding the olive oil a little at a time. Or simply place the tofu in a bowl and cream thoroughly. Add the garlic, then whisk in the olive oil a little at a time until smooth and thick. This keeps for only a day or two.

*Per serving: Calories: 232, Protein: 7 gm., Fat: 5 gm., Carbohydrates: 19 gm.*

# Red Wine Cream Sauce

*Try it over crêpes, loaves, casseroles or grains.*

Sauté the onions and celery in the oil or margarine until soft. Add the flour, cook 2 minutes, then add the hot stock and wine, stirring constantly. Add the chopped apple, cover, and simmer over low heat for 30 minutes. Strain out the vegetables. Add the mirin, soy sauce, miso, tomato paste, and salt to taste, and simmer for another 10 minutes. Add the soy milk and pepper to taste and heat thoroughly.

*Per 1/4 cup serving: Calories: 112, Protein: 2 gm., Fat: 6 gm., Carbohydrates: 11 gm.*

*Makes 2 cup*

1 small onion, minced

1 stalk celery, minced

3 Tbsp. oil or margarine

4 Tbsp. flour

1 3/4 cups hot stock

2/3 cup red wine

1 small apple, chopped

1 Tbsp. mirin

1 - 2 Tbsp. soy sauce

1 Tbsp. miso

1 - 2 Tbsp. tomato paste

salt to taste

1/3 cup or more rich soy milk or
    cream

pepper to taste

# Hot & Sweet Curry Sauce

*Makes individual servings*

*For each serving mix:*
*1 1/2 Tbsp. red wine vinegar*
*1 1/2 Tbsp. honey (more or less to*
  *taste)*
*2 tsp. Dijon-style mustard*
*1 tsp. curry powder*
*1 Tbsp. tahini (optional)*

*For six servings mix:*
*1/2 cup red wine vinegar*
*1/2 cup honey (more or less to*
  *taste)*
*1/4 cup Dijon-style mustard*
*2 Tbsp. curry powder*
*6 Tbsp. tahini (optional)*

*Great for steamed or sautéed vegetables or grains. It doesn't get any simpler than this!*

Mix up ingredients according to the number of servings desired.

*Per serving: Calories: 106, Protein: .5 gm., Fat: 1 gm., Carbohydrates: 27 gm.*

# *Pesto Sauce*

*Makes 2 cups*

*Pesto has become extremely popular in recent years, and understandably, since it is such a highly versatile sauce. It is a natural over pasta, but it can also be added to soup, tomato sauce, pizza, extended with vinegar as a salad dressing, or simply spread on bread. At the height of summer, I like to take advantage of the fresh basil that abounds in stores and make a large batch. It keeps for several weeks refrigerated or can be frozen for longer periods. Although a true Italian may frown upon you, by all means go ahead and use a blender!*

Combine everything in a blender or food processor and blend until a nice, thick green sauce is produced, but take care to leave some texture.

Store refrigerated in a jar with a coating of olive oil on top.

*Per 1 Tbsp. serving: Calories: 75, Protein: .5 gm., Fat: 8 gm., Carbohydrates: .5 gm.*

*2 packed cups fresh basil leaves*

*2 - 4 cloves garlic*

*1/2 cup plus 2 Tbsp. pine nuts*

*1 cup extra virgin olive oil*

*1 - 3 Tbsp. miso*

# A Good Bowl of Soup

Soups need no introduction; everybody loves them. Here you will find some new versions of traditional favorites, such as French Onion Soup, or Gazpacho, as well as some new and different ones, such as Chilled Curried Carrot and Fruit Soup,. All of them are sure to please.

A word about stocks: If you save your vegetable scraps and make a batch of stock every two or three weeks, you will always have some on hand for a pot of soup. If, however, making a stock from scratch seems too laborious, then go ahead and opt for a good quality packaged broth or bouillon, making sure that it is all-natural and contains no MSG. Natural food stores now carry a wide variety, and you willsurely find one that you like. Some are sodium-free, allowing you to control the saltiness of the soup. Also, match your stock with your soup; a tomato-based stock would be too strong for a delicate and sweet Carrot and Orange Soup, although perfect for Pesto Vegetable Soup. Follow the guidelines for making Basic Vegetable Stock or shop around until you find a packaged stock that you like.

# Basic Vegetable Stock

*The scraps of vegetables accumulating in your refrigerator will make a good vegetable stock. Save carrot tops, potato skins, scallion ends, and other bits and pieces and supplement them with a couple of sliced onions, carrots, and celery to fill a big soup pot for your own homemade stock. The following guidelines will help you in making and seasoning stocks for a variety of soups.*

*Fruits and vegetables suitable for any type stock:*

*apples, to add a slight sweetness*

*carrots, tops and all, sliced*

*celery, tops and all, sliced*

*cucumbers, peel if skin is bitter*

*garlic - you can add a whole head as the long simmering leaves only a mellow aroma*

*leeks, sliced (bottoms, too)*

*lettuce, an old head or wilted outer leaves*

*mushrooms, whole or just stems*

*onions, sliced (also skins of any color)*

*parsley, stems and all*

*parsnips, sliced*

*potatoes and potato peels*

*scallions, (bottoms, too)*

*zucchini, tops and all, sliced*

Onions, carrots, and celery are fairly essential to producing any stock. Use all or a combination of the vegetables and seasonings suggested above, filling a soup pot with them. Seasonings are optional—you can make a stock from just vegetables and water if desired. Add water to cover the vegetables. Cover with a tight-fitting lid and bring to a boil. Lower the heat and simmer gently for 1 to 2 hours, adding a little more water if necessary. Strain the stock and discard the vegetables. Taste and adjust the seasonings as desired. If it tastes weak, boil it down rapidly to concentrate it.

The stock can be used immediately or stored in the refrigerator or freezer for later use. If kept in the refrigerator, it should be brought to a boil at least once a week.

This recipe is for a non-fat vegetable stock. For a richer flavor, saute the onions, celery, and carrots in two to four tablespoons of vegetable oil until tender, then add the other vegetables, seasonings, and water, and proceed as in the above recipe.

For stronger flavored or "Italian"-type soups (minestrone, lentil, basil vegetable, tomato, etc.): in addition to the afore-mentioned vegetables and seasonings, tomatoes, fresh basil, rosemary, lots of garlic, and extra soy sauce may be added if desired.

Avoid vegetables from the cabbage family, such as broccoli, cabbage or cauliflower, since they are too strong unless used in making a broccoli or cabbage soup. Mild vegetables and varieties from the squash family (zucchini, pumpkin, etc.) may be added to the ones suggested above, however.

*Seasonings to be added as desired:*

*herbs and spices of choice - remember to keep in mind the soup you will make with it, otherwise, stay basic by using bay leaves, thyme, and parsley*

*miso - add a small amount— 1 to 2 tablespoons—for a richer flavor*

*nutritional yeast - several table-spoons will add a deep, hearty flavor*

*salt and pepper to taste*

*soy sauce - depending on soup, add anywhere from 2 tsp. to several tablespoons; adds a "meatier" flavor*

*wine or sherry - for a gourmet touch*

# Parsnip Stock

2 Tbsp. oil

2 large onions, sliced

2 medium carrots,
   sliced 1/4" thick

1 large parsnip, diced

2 stalks celery, sliced

2 bay leaves

1/2 tsp. celery seeds

1 large cucumber, peeled and
   diced (Japanese cucumbers do
   not need to be peeled)

2 quarts water

*This excellent stock is rich with a natural sweetness. It is a fine replacement for chicken stock.*

Heat the oil in a large pot. Sauté the first four vegetables, covered, for ten minutes. Add the remaining vegetables and water, cover, and bring to a boil. Lower heat and simmer gently for 1 1/2 hours. Strain, pressing the juices out of the vegetables. If the flavor seems week, boil rapidly, uncovered, to reduce by 10% to 20%.

# *Shiitake Consommé*

The meaty depth of the shiitake and their broth is nicely rounded out by the
sweetness of red bell peppers. This is a nice soup to serve at the start of a
rich meal.

Soak the shiitake in the water for 3 to 4 hours. Cut off the
stems with a sharp knife and slice very thinly. Combine the
shiitake stock, sliced shiitake, sliced mushrooms, red wine,
soy sauce, and consommé or bouillon cubes in a pot and
simmer, covered, for 30 minutes. Add the red peppers and
continue to simmer for another 15 minutes. Season with
freshly ground black pepper and add the parsley just before
serving.

This soup can be made up to two hours ahead of serving,
but is best if served as soon as possible.

*Per serving: Calories: 52, Protein: 3 gm., Fat: 0 gm., Carbohydrates:14 gm.*

*Serves 6-8*

*See photo on page 99.*

*15 - 20 dried shiitake mushrooms*

*8 cups water*

*8 oz. mushrooms, sliced*

*1 1/2 cups red wine*

*3 Tbsp. soy sauce*

*2 vegetable consommé or bouillon
   cubes*

*2 medium red bell peppers,
   sliced into thin rings*

*plenty of freshly grated black
   pepper*

*1/3 cup finely chopped parsley*

# Cucumber Vichyssoise

Serves 4

2 cups cucumbers, diced
 (preferably Japanese or
 European seedless variety)
1/3 cup onions, chopped
3/4 cup potatoes, diced
2 cups vegetable stock
1/2 cup soy milk
1/2 cup soy yogurt or soy sour
 cream, pages 19-20
salt and pepper to taste

*A refreshing vichyssoise with the addition of cucumbers. Serve it on a hot day.*

Peel the cucumbers if their skins are bitter or waxed. Place the vegetables and stock in a covered pot and cook until soft, about ten or fifteen minutes. Purée in a blender or food processor. Add the soy milk and yogurt or sour cream, season with salt and pepper, and refrigerate until thoroughly chilled. Garnish with a few slivers of cucumber.

*Per serving: Calories: 65, Protein: 5 gm., Fat: 2 gm., Carbohydrates: 9 gm.*

# Quick Avocado and Cucumber Soup

*Serves 4*

*This delicate soup can be whipped up in minutes. If you don't have time to chill it, add ice cubes!*

Sauté the onion in the oil, covered, until soft. Combine the onion with all the other ingredients except the soy milk or cream in a blender and whip until smooth and creamy. Mix in the soy milk or cream and season with salt and pepper to taste. Chill thoroughly before serving, if possible. If all the ingredients are cold, the soup should chill in a couple of hours. Do not let it stand overnight as the avocado will cause the soup to change color. To help prevent discoloration, place saran wrap directly on top of the soup.

*Per serving: Calories: 204, Protein: 5 gm., Fat: 8 gm., Carbohydrates: 13 gm.*

1 small onion, chopped

1 Tbsp. oil or margarine

1 1/2 ripe avocados,
    pitted and diced

1 large cucumber,
    peeled and diced

2 Tbsp. white wine

3 Tbsp. orange juice

2 Tbsp. lemon juice

1 cup stock, chilled

1 cup soy milk or cream

salt and pepper to taste

# Gazpacho

*Serves 4-6*

4 very ripe tomatoes, diced

1 Japanese cucumber with peel
    intact, diced,
      or 1/2 salad cucumber, diced
      (peeled if skin is bitter or
      waxed)

1/2 bell pepper, green, red, or
    yellow, diced

1/2 medium onion, diced

1 to 2 cloves garlic

1 cup stock

1 to 3 Tbsp. red wine vinegar

1 to 2 Tbsp. good olive oil
    (optional)

2 Tbsp. red wine (optional)

salt and pepper to taste

Topping: *finely chopped
    tomatoes, onions, peppers,
    cucumbers, and, if desired,
    capers and croûtons*

*Here is my version of the famous Spanish soup that is so good during summertime when vegetables are at their sweetest.*

Blend all the ingredients in a food processor or blender to desired consistency—some like it absolutely smooth while others like to leave some texture. Chill thoroughly and pass the various toppings around at serving time.

*Per serving: Calories: 39, Protein: 2 gm., Fat: 0 gm., Carbohydrates: 8 gm.*

# Chilled Carrot and Orange Soup

Serves 6-8

*I was once asked to prepare a dinner where every dish served had to contain carrots as the main ingredient. Here is the unusual and refreshing soup I created for that hot summer day.*

In a covered saucepan sauté the onions and carrots in the oil or margarine for about 10 minutes, stirring frequently. Add the stock, diced potato, and orange peel. Cover and simmer gently until the vegetables are soft. Add the wine and continue cooking for five more minutes to take the edge off the wine. Allow to cool. Purée until smooth, then add the soy milk or cream. Add the freshly squeezed orange juice a little at a time, checking the flavor all the while. It should taste pleasantly sweet but not like juice. Season with salt and pepper and chill for several hours before serving.

*Per serving: Calories : 104, Protein: 3 gm., Fat: 5 gm., Carbohydrates: 13 gm.*

1 medium onion, sliced

1 lb. carrots, sliced

2 Tbsp. oil or margarine

3 1/2 cups stock

1 small potato, peeled or scrubbed
    well, and diced

3 strips orange peel, 1/2" wide
    and 2" long

1/4 cup white wine

1 cup soy milk or cream
    (more if necessary)

juice of 1/2 orange (or less)

salt and white pepper to taste

# Chilled Curried Carrot and Fruit Soup

Serves 4-6

See photo on page 99.

1 medium onion, sliced

1 Tbsp. margarine

6 oz. potatoes (approx. 1 med.),
    preferably new or waxy-type,
    peeled and diced

1 cup stock

12 oz. carrot juice, freshly
    squeezed or canned

8 oz. tropical fruit juice,
    unsweetened (preferably
    containing pineapple, orange
    and banana juice)

1 tsp. curry powder (or more,
    depending on strength)

1 cup rich soy milk

*A delectable soup that is slightly spicy and sweet at the same time. Simple to make because it uses carrot and fruit juices, it is quite unique and will surely stimulate appetites.*

Sauté the onion in the margarine in a covered saucepan until soft. Add the potatoes, stock, juices, curry powder, and salt to taste. Bring to a boil, cover, and simmer gently for 20 minutes, or until the vegetables are very soft. Allow to cool a bit before puréeing. Place in a blender or food processor and purée until very smooth. Chill thoroughly, then add the soy milk and chill for another hour or so before serving. Adjust seasonings as necessary, adding more salt or curry. If desired, swirl some soy cream or cashew cream in each portion as garnish.

*Per serving: Calories: 138, Protein: 5 gm., Fat: 3 gm., Carbohydrates: 23 gm.*

# Chilled Spiced Autumn Soup

*A new twist on pumpkin soup, as good on a summer's eve as in the autumn.*

Sauté the onion, celery, and garlic in the oil until soft. Add the stock, squash, yam, nutmeg, and ginger. Cover and cook until very soft. Purée until smooth in a food processor or blender. Add the soymilk, season to taste with salt and pepper, and chill overnight or for several hours before serving.

*Per serving: Calories: 298, Protein: 8 gm., Fat: 3 gm., Carbohydrates: 62 gm.*

*Serves 4-6*

*1 large onion, sliced*

*1 stalk celery, sliced*

*2 cloves garlic, crushed*

*1 Tbsp. oil*

*1 1/2 qts. Parsnip Stock, page 90*

*1 1/2 lbs. banana squash, kabocha (Japanese pumpkin), acorn squash, or pumpkin, peeled and cut into slices or chunks*

*1 lb. yams, peeled and sliced or diced*

*4 - 6 slivers fresh ginger (1/2" x 1" x 1/8")*

*1/2 tsp. nutmeg*

*1/2 cup soy or cashew milk*

*salt and pepper*

# Clear Garlic Soup with Mushrooms

*Serves 4-6*

*A highly unusual and delicious soup. Do not be put off by the idea of using 4 to 5 entire bulbs of garlic for this soup, because the simmering leaves only a mellow flavor. Of course, garlic lovers can always increase the quantity of garlic added at the end.*

*4 large bulbs garlic*

*10 - 12 dried shiitake,*
*    reconstituted*

*1 lb. mushrooms, sliced thinly*
*    or 2/3 lbs. mushrooms and 1/3*
*    lb. shimeji oyster mushrooms*

*3 Tbsp. olive oil*

*8 cups stock (part or all may be*
*    shiitake stock)*

*3 to 4 pinches saffron*

*3 - 4 Tbsp. soy sauce*

*3/4 cup red wine*

*an extra 6 to 8 cloves garlic,*
*    finely minced*

*salt and pepper to taste*

*minced parsley for garnish*

Separate the 4 heads of garlic into cloves and dunk in boiling water for 30 seconds. The skins should slip off easily. Discard the skins and simmer the cloves of garlic in the stock for 10 to 15 minutes until very tender. Strain and discard the garlic.

Slice the shiitake thinly and sauté in a covered pan with the mushrooms and shimeji oyster mushrooms (if you are using them) in the olive oil for 5 minutes. Add the garlic, stock, saffron, soy sauce, red wine, and the minced garlic, and simmer for 15 to 20 minutes. Adjust flavorings, adding more garlic, saffron, or soy sauce as desired. Season with salt and pepper, and garnish each bowl of soup with a sprinkling of parsley.

*Per serving: Calories: 140, Protein: 3 gm., Fat: 8 gm., Carbohydrates: 9 gm.*

*Clockwise from top left: Shiitake Consommé, pg. 91, Chilled Curried Carrot and Fruit Soup, pg. 96, Cold Cream of Watercress and Apple Soup, pg. 107*

# French Onion Soup

Serves 4-6

*The sweetness of onions really comes through in this rich and hearty soup. It is excellent by itself, but feel free to serve it "au gratin" with a slice of thick French bread and cheese (soy, of course). The secret to excellent onion soup lies in the slow cooking and browning of the onions, so take your time with this soup.*

Heat the oil and margarine in a large dutch oven or soup pot with a heavy bottom. Add the onions, cover, and cook slowly over low heat for 20 minutes, stirring frequently. Add the honey and salt, uncover, and continue to cook for another 30 minutes until the onions are sweet and nicely browned. This browning process is very important. Add the stock and wine and simmer partially covered for 30 minutes. Add the soy sauce and brandy and continue simmering for another 15 minutes. Add salt, pepper, a little more soy sauce, and brandy to taste, if necessary, being sure to simmer for several minutes after adding. Serve with a sprinkling of parsley to garnish or "au gratin"—topped with a "croûte," i.e., French bread, baked in a slow oven until dry, a thick slab of soy cheese, and placed under the broiler until the cheese melts.

*Per serving: Calories: 241, Protein: 7 gm., Fat: 5 gm., Carbohydrates: 39 gm.*

1 Tbsp. each oil and margarine

3 lbs. onions, sliced

1 tsp. honey

1 tsp. salt

1 1/2 to 2 quarts stock

1/2 cup white or red wine

3 Tbsp. soy sauce

3 Tbsp. brandy or cognac

salt and pepper to taste,
    if necessary

parsley to garnish

stale or lightly toasted slices of
    French bread and soy cheese
    (optional)

*Tofu Bourguignon, pgs. 138-9*

# Fresh Tomato and Bread Soup

*Serves 2-3*

2 Tbsp. extra virgin olive oil

4 - 5 cloves garlic, finely minced

1 1/2 lbs. very ripe tomatoes,
  chopped

2 cups hot stock

1/3 cup fresh basil leaves, packed,
  or 2 tsp. dried basil and
  several springs fresh parsley

salt and pepper to taste

3 - 4 slices French bread,
  1/2" thick

*Use red, ripe (even overly ripe) tomatoes for this delightful repast that is sure to capture the flavors of summer's bounty. Made in just minutes, it is the perfect soup to make for a romantic dinner for two with pasta and a chilled white wine. For a larger crowd, double the recipe.*

Heat the olive oil in a pot and sauté the garlic over low heat for 3-4 minutes. Add the tomatoes, turn the heat up to high, and bring to a boil. Reduce heat and simmer for five minutes. Add the stock and basil (plus parsley if dried basil is used) and continue simmering uncovered for about ten minutes, until the tomatoes are tender but still fresh tasting (do not overcook). Season with salt and pepper. Tear the bread into large chunks and stir into the soup. Cover and allow to sit for at least five minutes before serving.

*Per serving: Calories: 247, Protein: 6 gm., Fat: 11 gm., Carbohydrates: 30 gm.*

# Pesto Vegetable Soup

*Flavorful pesto sauce makes a lively brew out of a pot of fresh summer vegetables. Best if freshly picked vegetables from your garden are used, but perfectly satisfying using whatever you can find in the produce section along with some frozen peas and beans.*

Place the onions, carrot, mushrooms, tomatoes, and potatoes in a large pot and add the stock. Cover and bring to a boil, then lower the heat and simmer gently for about 15 minutes. Add the broccoli, green beans, peas, zucchini, and small white beans and continue cooking until the vegetables are soft. Add the soy sauce and pesto and turn off the heat. Grate plenty of fresh pepper and check the flavoring. You may want to add more pesto. Serve with a crusty bread to soak up the tasty broth.

*Per serving: Calories: 227, Protein: 9 gm., Fat: 9 gm., Carbohydrates: 30 gm.*

*Makes a big pot of soup—enough to serve 10 or 12*

2 medium onions, chopped

1 carrot, sliced or diced as desired

3/4 lb. mushrooms, quartered

1 1/2 lbs. red ripe tomatoes, chopped

1 lb. waxy new or red potatoes, diced

2 quarts stock

1 large stalk broccoli, cut into small florets, stalk peeled and sliced

1 cup diced string beans

1 cup fresh or frozen peas

1 large or 2 small zucchini, sliced 1/4" thick

1 cup cooked small white beans

1 Tbsp. soy sauce

1/2 cup or more Pesto Sauce, page 85

lots of freshly grated pepper

*Note: Other vegetables that are good to use are cauliflower, eggplants, leeks, bell peppers, snow peas, etc. Use whatever you have or can get.*

# Genna's Homemade Soup

*Serves 2-3*

*This is the first vegetarian dish I ever learned to make—at the tender age of 12. Although it makes use of canned goods and is extremely simple, I have included it here because it is so tasty and nostalgic. The recipe was created and given to me by a classmate, Genna, whose entire family was vegetarian. I thought it was tasty then, and still do now, and thank her for this dish which I have made hundreds of times. Although the original recipe calls for using a 1/3 cup of butter, I have taken the liberty of reducing it to a tablespoon or two of olive oil. This is a dish even a child can make.*

*1 onion, finely chopped*

*1 - 2 Tbsp. olive oil*

*1 (15 oz.) can kidney beans*

*1 (15 oz.) can stewed tomatoes*

*2 tsp. mixed herbs  (basil, thyme, rosemary, oregano, etc.)*

*salt and pepper to taste*

*2 cups cooked fettucine or Tofu Pasta, pages 142-3 (optional)*

*dash cayenne pepper (optional)*

Heat the oil in a saucepan. Add the onions, cover, and sauté until tender. Add the beans, tomatoes, and herbs, cover again, and cook for 10 to 15 minutes. Season with salt and pepper. Serve as is, or ladle into soup bowls over fettucine or Tofu Pasta.

*Per serving: Calories: 230, Protein: 10 gm., Fat: 6 gm., Carbohydrates: 34 gm.*

# Chestnut Soup with Apple Garnish

*A warm and wintery soup for Thanksgiving or Christmas.*

In a large covered pot sauté the vegetables and chestnuts in 2 tablespoons of the margarine for 5 to 6 minutes. Add the stock and simmer for 20 minutes until the vegetables are soft. Purée in a blender or food processor until smooth. Add the soy cream or milk and season with salt and pepper. Add the brandy. Reheat gently but do not allow to boil.

Chop the apple into small pieces and sauté over relatively high heat in the remaining tablespoon of margarine. Sprinkle with nutmeg. Top each serving with the apples at serving time.

*Per serving: Calories: 255, Protein: 6 gm., Fat: 8 gm., Carbohydrates: 39 gm.*

*Serves 4-6*

*12 oz. chestnut meats (from 1 1/2 lbs. fresh), shelled and cooked (canned or bottled can be substituted and are easier to use)*

*1 large onion, sliced*
*1 medium carrot, sliced*
*3 Tbsp. margarine*
*3 to 3 1/2 cups stock*
*1 1/2 cups soy milk or cream*
*salt and pepper to taste*
*1 - 2 Tbsp. brandy*
*1 apple*
*freshly grated nutmeg*

# Creamy Mushroom and Red Wine Soup

Serves 6.

1 Tbsp. oil or margarine

2 onions, chopped

2 cloves garlic, crushed

1 3/4 cups red wine

1 1/2 lbs. mushrooms, sliced

4 1/2 cups soy milk

1/2 tsp. tarragon

3 Tbsp. powdered broth
   or 3 - 4 cubes bouillon

salt and pepper to taste

additional 1/4 cup red wine

*Rich, deep, and delicious.*

Sauté onions and garlic in the oil, covered, until soft. Add the red wine and simmer, uncovered, for 5-7 minutes. Add the mushrooms, soy milk, broth, and tarragon, and simmer, partially covered, for 30 minutes. Purée in a food processor, leaving some texture. Return to the pot and season with salt and pepper and the final 1/4 cup of wine, reheating gently.

*Per serving: Calories: 189, Protein: 10 gm., Fat: 5 gm., Carbohydrates: 17 gm.*

# Cold Cream of Watercress and Apple Soup

*This is one of my favorite soups. My good friend, Jamelia Saied, an excellent chef and an inspiration to all, first made this soup for me one wonderful Christmas Eve at her home. I immediately went back to my kitchen and tried to figure out the recipe. Here is my vegan version.*

Sauté the onions and celery in the margarine in a large pot over low heat for five minutes. Add the potatoes and stock, cover, and simmer gently until the vegetables are soft. Add the thinly sliced apple and continue cooking for another 3 or 4 minutes. Add the watercress and cook only another minute or two until the watercress wilts. Remove from the heat and purée in a blender or food processor until completely green and creamy—this may take a few minutes. Chill thoroughly. Add the soy milk or cream, and chill for another 1/2 hour. Before serving grate the apple and add it to the soup. Garnish with watercress springs and thin slices of apple if you like.

*Per serving: Calories: 152, Protein: 6 gm., Fat: 7 gm., Carbohydrates: 19 gm.*

*Serves 6-8*

*See photo on page 99.*

2 medium onions, sliced

2 stalks celery, sliced thinly

3 Tbsp. margarine

4 small potatoes, scrubbed well
   and peeled, if desired, and
   diced

6 cups stock (Parsnip Stock, page
   90, works well for this)

1/4 apple, sliced thinly

2 cups watercress, packed

2 cups rich soy milk or cream

1 large or 2 small crisp, sweet
   apples, grated

## QUICK AND TASTY TOFU CREAM SOUPS

Almost any vegetables can be creamed with tofu to make tasty, low-calorie soups that contain no added fat, flour, or other thickening agent. I love these soups because they are not only easy to make but don't taste like diet food! Here are several versions, all of which can be served hot or cold. Try other vegetables as well and create your own soups.

# Cream of Pumpkin Soup

Serves 4

*You might want to try using Japanese pumpkin, or kabocha. The meat is richer and sweeter than American pumpkins.*

Peel the pumpkin or kabocha, chop into 1" chunks, and cook with the onion in the stock until tender, about fifteen minutes. Purée the tofu and soy milk in a blender until perfectly creamy. Transfer to another dish. Without washing the blender pour in the soup mixture and purée until smooth. Pour this back into the pot and mix in the tofu purée. Chill thoroughly if you are going to serve it cold; otherwise, heat gently, but do not allow it to boil or it will curdle. Season to taste with salt, pepper, and nutmeg.

*Per serving: Calories: 128,  Protein:  8 gm., Fat: 3 gm.,  Carbohydrates: 19 gm.*

1 lb. pumpkin pulp, banana
   squash, or kabocha

1/2 medium onion, sliced

2 1/2 cups stock

8 oz. tofu

1/2 cup soy milk

2 Tbsp. white wine

salt, pepper, and nutmeg to taste

# Cream of Corn Soup

*Serves 4*

8 oz. frozen corn

1/2 medium onion, sliced

2 1/2 cups stock

8 oz. tofu

1/2 cup soy milk

2 Tbsp. white wine

salt and pepper to taste

*Substitute corn for the pumpkin in the Cream of Pumpkin Soup.*

Cook according to the Cream of Pumpkin soup recipe on page 109, using the ingredients listed here.

*Per serving: Calories: 119, Protein: 8 gm., Fat: 3 gm., Carbohydrates: 16 gm.*

# Cream of Green Pea Soup

Follow the Cream of Pumpkin Soup recipe on page 109, using the ingredients listed here.

For this soup the amount of tofu and soy milk may be decreased if desired. This soup is especially good chilled.

*Per serving: Calories: 120, Protein: 8 gm., Fat: 3 gm., Carbohydrates: 15 gm.*

*Serves 4*

*8 oz. frozen or fresh peas*

*1/2 medium onion, sliced*

*2 1/2 cups stock*

*8 oz. tofu*

*1/2 cup soy milk*

*2 Tbsp. white wine*

*1 tsp. honey*

*salt and pepper to taste*

# Entreés to Get Excited About

## A Collection of Both the Rich and Simple for Entertaining and Family Dining

These recipes range from the very simple to the highly elaborate. All the them are extremely good. Gone are the heavy, beany vegetarian creations of yore and "gourmet" efforts relying heavily on cheese and eggs. The following recipes are delicious, not simply as vegetarian food, but as food in itself.

As the weather begins to cool in the fall, serve the wonderful Chestnut Cabbage Rolls with Red Wine Sauce or make some Tofu Fettucine and serve it with Tofu Bourguignon. For that really special dinner try French Moussaka with Rich Brown Sauce and on Thanksgiving, the fantastic and fun Great Gluten Turkey with dressing and gravy, surrounded by Garlic Rice and Minted Carrots. For a simple winter repast, try the Herbed Soybean Casserole with some homemade whole grain bread, and for a late night feast, Pasta with Three Mushrooms. Whatever the mood and occasion, you will find a recipe here to suit it.

# Wild Rice Crêpes

*Serves 4-6*

*Thank goodness wild rice is really not a rice at all, but a type of grass. If it were rice, I would have had to smuggle it into Japan all those years I lived there in order to enjoy it in luscious dishes such as these crêpes. Serve with Nutty Almond Sauce or Rich Brown Sauce, pages 63 and 74, for a gourmet entrée.*

*8 - 12 eggless crêpes, page 146*

Prepare the crêpes as described on page 146 (or according to your favorite recipe). If you have a supply stored in your freezer, take them out to defrost.

*3/4 cup wild rice, uncooked*

*2 3/4 cups stock*

*1/4 medium onion, finely minced*

Place the wild rice with the stock and the finely minced onion in a saucepan with a tight fitting lid. Turn the heat up to high. After it comes to a boil, turn it to low and cook for about an hour, or until all the liquid is gone and the rice is tender.

*2 stalks celery, thinly sliced*

*2 Tbsp. vegetable oil*

*3/4 medium onion,*
*    roughly chopped*

*1/4 lb. mushrooms, thickly sliced*

*5 to 6 shiitake mushrooms,*
*    fresh or reconstituted*
*    (page 18), cut into quarters*
*    or eighths*

*1/2 cup oyster mushrooms,*
*    separated into small clumps*
*    or other mushrooms*
*    (chanterelles or morels)*

*1 large tomato, chopped*

*1/2 tsp. sage, powdered*

*1 Tbsp. soy sauce*

*salt and pepper to taste*

While the rice is cooking, sauté the sliced celery in a couple of tablespoons of oil until relatively tender. Add the roughly chopped onion, mushrooms, shiitake, and oyster mushrooms, and continue sautéing until the vegetables are relatively soft. Add the cooked rice, the chopped tomato, sage, soy sauce, salt, and pepper, and continue to cook for another ten or fifteen minutes. Fill the crêpes with the mixture, roll up, and heat for ten minutes in a 350° oven before serving. Serve with Nutty Almond Sauce, page 63, Rich Brown Sauce, page 74, or Madeira Mushroom Sauce, page 73.

*Per serving: Calories: 384, Protein: 12 gm., Fat: 13 gm., Carbohydrates: 55 gm*

# Mediterranean Eggplant and Tofu Gratin

*Great for those occasions when only something hearty, "meaty," and Italian-tasting with garlic and herbal overtones will satisfy. Serve with crusty French bread and a big salad. This also makes wonderful leftovers.*

If you have time, it's a good idea to salt the eggplant to remove the bitter flavor and keep it from absorbing too much oil. Slice the eggplant into 3/8" thick rounds, sprinkle liberally with salt, and place in a colander to drain for 20 to 30 minutes. Scrape the surface with a knife or rinse quickly and pat dry with paper towels. Leave a little salt clinging to the eggplant, as it enhances the flavor. Heat a couple of tablespoons of olive oil in a skillet and sauté the eggplant slices on both sides until golden brown and tender. Set aside.

Wipe out the skillet. Mix the soy sauce, peanut butter, tomato paste, water, and cayenne pepper together in a bowl. Crumble or shred the tofu so it resembles large breadcrumbs, and mix it with the soy-peanut butter marinade, squeezing with your hands so that the tofu absorbs it all. In the same skillet heat two more tablespoons of olive oil and sauté the tofu until well-browned, stirring constantly.

Slice the tomatoes 3/8" thick. In a 10" shallow gratin or casserole dish, put down a layer of the sautéed eggplants, using up half of them. Spread the browned tofu over them, then cover with a layer of half the tomatoes. Sprinkle on half the minced garlic, a little salt, and a half-teaspoon of rosemary. Add another layer of eggplant, then the rest of the tomatoes. Sprinkle with more garlic, rosemary, and a little salt, if desired. Fresh basil leaves can also be added.

Bake in a preheated 375° oven for 45 to 50 minutes.

*Per serving: Calories: 512, Protein: 21 gm., Fat: 27 gm., Carbohydrates: 50gm.*

Serves 4

1 1/3 lbs. eggplant
    (approx. 1 medium)
2 Tbsp. olive oil

2 Tbsp. soy sauce
2 Tbsp. peanut butter
2 Tbsp. tomato paste
3 - 4 Tbsp. water
2 - 3 dashes cayenne pepper
1 lb. frozen tofu, thawed and
    squeezed dry (see page 23)
2 Tbsp. olive oil

1 1/3 lbs. fresh, ripe tomatoes
    (approx. 3 1/2 medium)
3 to 6 cloves garlic, or more,
    minced or pressed
1 tsp. dried rosemary
salt to taste
fresh basil to decorate (optional)

# Savory Stuffed Onions

Serves 6

6 large onions

2 Tbsp. margarine

1 cup cashews, ground in a
    blender or food processor

1 3/4 cups cooked long-grain
    brown rice ,
    or brown basmati rice (for
    slightly  nuttier flavor)

1/2 cup parsley, chopped

1 1/4 tsp. dried sage, rubbed

salt and pepper to taste

1/2 cup white wine

1/2 cup good stock

1/2 cup rich soy milk or cream,
    or almond milk (optional)

*These can be made a day or two ahead and baked an hour or so before serving. If you have the time, make the Tangy White Wine Sauce to serve with it. A simpler sauce can be made by adding some soy milk or cream to the basting liquid, as explained below.*

You can save yourself the tears when dealing with onions if you refrigerate them at least overnight or soak them in cold water for thirty minutes after you peel them. Cut a slice off the top and bottom of each onion. The onions should then sit upright without rolling over. With a tablespoon-size measuring spoon or a melon ball scooper, remove the insides of the onions from the top, leaving a wall 1/3" thick all around. Chop this pulp finely and set it aside.

Place the onion shells in a stove top steamer, or covered dish in a microwave, and cook until a fork pierces easily through the sides but the onions still retain their shape. They should not be allowed to become mushy. Allow to cool before handling.

Melt the margarine in a large skillet and sauté the chopped onion pulp, covered, until tender. Mix with the ground cashews, brown rice, sage, parsley, and salt and pepper to taste. If the mixture seems dry, a little soy or almond milk can be added, but the sautéed onions should provide enough moisture, especially if they were covered while being cooked.

Stuff the cooked and cooled onions with the rice and cashew mixture. Place the onions in a shallow casserole or gratin dish and pour the stock and white wine around them. Cover loosely with aluminum foil and bake in a 425° oven for 20 minutes. Then turn down the oven to 375° and continue baking for another 40 minutes, removing the aluminum foil during the last 20 minutes to allow the tops to brown. If you find that the onions are not browning during that period, pour the liquid from the baking dish into a saucepan and continue baking the onions "dry."

For the sauce, either make and serve Tangy White Wine Sauce, page 68, or add the soy or almond milk to the remaining cooking liquid and simmer for a few minutes in a saucepan to let flavors mingle and thicken slightly.

*Per serving: Calories: 324, Protein: 10 gm., Fat: 15 gm., Carbohydrates: 41 gm.*

# Tofu Burgers Suprême

*Makes 4 large burgers*

*This is what convinced my younger brother that vegetarian food could be delicious. Because frozen tofu is used, these burgers are nice and chewy. Try them with a sauce, such as the Easy Brown Mushroom Sauce, page 77, or leftover Rich Brown Sauce, page 74. They taste great in a bun or pita with all the fixin's, too!*

*1/2 cup onion, finely chopped*

*1/3 cup mushrooms, chopped*

*1/3 cup celery, finely chopped*

In a covered pan sauté the onions, mushrooms, and celery in a small amount of water until tender. The vegetables can also be microwaved until tender, using no oil.

*1 lb. frozen tofu, thawed and*
   *squeezed dry*

*1 to 2 cloves garlic, minced*

*2 Tbsp. soy sauce*

*2 - 3 tsp. miso*

*2 - 3 Tbsp. tomato paste*

*2 - 3 Tbsp. tahini or sesame paste*

*3 - 4 Tbsp. water*

*3/4 cup breadcrumbs*

*1/2 cup parsley, chopped*

Squeeze the water out of the defrosted tofu and shred it into little bits. Mix with the vegetables, garlic, soy sauce, miso, and tomato paste. Thin the tahini with the water to produce a smooth, thick, white sauce that will bind the mixture. Add it to the tofu and vegetable mixture, mix well, and add the breadcrumbs and parsley. The mixture should be moist but not too wet, and firm enough to form into patties. Cook in a lightly oiled pan over low heat until browned on both sides. Don't cover while cooking or some of chewiness will be lost.

*Per serving: Calories: 227, Protein: 15 gm., Fat: 9 gm., Carbohydrates: 24 gm.*

# Creamy Tempeh Curry

A mild, slightly sweet, and creamy curry sauce covers morsels of tempeh, raisins, and vegetables. Make it hotter by increasing the amount of curry powder used. Serve with brown rice or Garlic Rice, page 195.

Sauté the onions in the oil until relatively tender, then add the grated tempeh and sauté several more minutes until the onion is completely soft. Add the curry powder and cook another two minutes. Add the tomatoes and stock, cover, and bring to a simmer. Add the green beans and raisins, cover again, and lower heat to simmer gently for 10 to 15 minutes. Add the soy or coconut milk and cook a few more minutes to thicken. If your soy or coconut milk is on the thin side, you can thicken it by adding a little arrowroot, kuzu, or cornstarch dissolved in a small amount of water. Season with salt, pepper, and more curry powder as desired.

*Per serving: Calories: 312, Protein: 17 gm., Fat: 14 gm., Carbohydrates: 30 gm.*

Serves 4

1 large onion, minced

2 Tbsp. oil or ghee
   (clarified margarine)

8 oz. tempeh, grated or finely
   chopped

1 1/4 Tbsp. curry powder

1 large or two medium ripe
   tomatoes, chopped

2 cups good stock

1 cup green beans, cut into
   1/2" lengths

1/2 cup raisins (more or less
   depending on how sweet a dish
   you prefer)

1 cup or more rich soy milk
   or  soy cream, (see page 19)
   or coconut milk

salt and pepper to taste

# Vol-au-Vent with Three Mushrooms

*Serves 4 - 6*

*See photo on page  183.*

*4 shallot onions, minced*

*1/2 red bell pepper, chopped*

*2 Tbsp. margarine*

*20 oz. any combination of three*
*varieties of mushrooms*
*(fresh shiitake, oyster, button,*
*morels, chanterelles) etc.,*
*sliced or torn, depending the*
*variety used*

*6 Tbsp. flour*

*2 cups Tangy White Wine Sauce,*
*page 68*

*1/2 cup chopped parsley*

*4 - 6 pastry or Vol-au-Vent shells*

*1 - 2 cups extra wine sauce for*
*pouring around*

*You can use any three types of wild mushrooms for this dish.*

Sauté the shallots and red pepper in the margarine until tender. Add the mushrooms to the shallots and sauté until the mushrooms are tender. Add the flour to the sautéed vegetables and cook for 2 - 3 minutes. Combine the white wine sauce with the mushrooms and shallots and cook until thick, then add the chopped parsley and cook for another minute. Immediately pour the creamed mixture into 4 - 6 hot pastry or Vol-au-Vent shells. Serve on individual plates with additional wine sauce poured around.

*Per serving: Calories: 380, Protein: 12 gm., Fat: 12 gm.,Carbohydrates: 62 gm.*

# Tempeh Mexicali

*Great with Garlic Rice or as a filling for enchiladas or tacos.*

Heat the olive oil in a large skillet. Add the cumin seeds and cayenne or red pepper, starting with 1/4 teaspoon, and allow to sizzle for a moment. Add the onions and garlic and sauté until relatively soft. Add the tempeh and continue to cook, stirring frequently, for another 5 minutes. Meanwhile, chop the tomatoes finely and add them to the pan along with the mushrooms. Cover and cook for 30 minutes. Flavor with soy sauce, salt, pepper, and additional cayenne as desired, cooking another minute or two to allow flavors to mingle. Top with Tofu Sour Cream and serve along with Garlic Rice, page 195.

*Per serving: Calories: 221, Protein: 12 gm., Fat: 11 gm., Carbohydrates: 18 gm.*

*Serves 4*

2 Tbsp. olive oil

1 tsp. whole cumin seeds

cayenne or red pepper to taste

1 large onion, chopped

3 - 4 cloves garlic, minced

6 oz. tempeh, shredded
   or crumbled

5 very ripe tomatoes,
   or 1 (32 oz.) can tomatoes

1/4 lb. mushrooms, halved

1 Tbsp. soy sauce

salt and freshly ground pepper
   to taste


Tofu Sour Cream, page 179,
   to serve alongside or on top

# Sweet and Sour Tofu

Serves 4 - 6

*Here is a vegetarian version of sweet and sour pork. Deep-fried tofu cutlets (called "atsuage" in Japanese) are first marinated, then baked until chewy before being combined with vegetables and a sauce sweetened primarily with apple juice.*

2 (12 oz.) blocks atsuage
  (the deep fried tofu available
  in Oriental groceries and some
  supermarkets - also sold as
  tofu "cutlets")

If you are unable to buy atsuage ready-made, you can deep-fat fry pressed or firm blocks of tofu at 375° for 3 - 5 minutes until golden brown. Drain well.

Cut the deep-fried tofu into 1" chunks. Mix the ingredients for the marinade and marinate the tofu in it for 2 hours, basting or turning the pieces over occasionally. Bake on a greased cookie sheet for 30 - 35 minutes in a 350° oven, or until brown and chewy.

Sauté the onion in oil until tender but still crisp. Add the carrots, shiitake, and green peppers, and sauté 3 to 4 minutes. Add the pineapple along with all the ingredients for the

Marinade for tofu:
3 1/2 Tbsp. cider or rice vinegar
1 tsp. tomato paste
2 Tbsp. sake or sherry (optional)
2 Tbsp. mirin
1 Tbsp. soy sauce
salt and pepper to taste

Vegetables:
1 large onion, cut into eighths
  and separated into leaves
1 Tbsp. oil
1 small carrot, cut into sticks
  or slices
4 - 8 shiitake mushrooms, fresh
  or reconstituted, cut into
  halves or fourths
1 green pepper, cut into 1"
  squares
1 cup pineapple chunks

Sweet and Sour Sauce *except* the kuzu or arrowroot and simmer gently for 10 minutes to allow flavors to mingle. Add the baked tofu. Dissolve the arrowroot or kuzu in water and add slowly in a steady stream while stirring constantly until the sauce is thick and has a glazed appearance. If too thin, add more kuzu or arrowroot.

Serve with brown rice. If desired, a little chopped cilantro may be sprinkled on top.

*Per serving: Calories: 354, Protein: 13 gm., Fat: 9 gm., Carbohydrates: 60 gm.*

*Sweet and Sour Sauce:*

*2 1/4 cups apple juice*

*3 Tbsp. tomato paste*

*1/2 cup rice or cider vinegar\**

*3 1/2 Tbsp. soy sauce*

*3 Tbsp. honey*

*1 - 2 Tbsp. mirin*

*1 - 2 tsp. or more miso*
   *(optional—it will add some*
   *depth to the flavor)*

*1 Tbsp. kuzu,*
   *or 2-3 Tbsp. arrowroot or*
   *cornstarch dissolved in small*
   *amount of water*

*\*Rice vinegar is milder and*
   *sweeter than cider vinegar. If*
   *you use cider vinegar, reduce*
   *the amount slightly.*

# Whole Cabbage with Hearty Tempeh Stuffing

*Serves 6-8*

1 medium head cabbage
  (approx. 2 lbs.)

12 oz. tempeh, minced or
  crumbled

3 Tbsp. cider vinegar

2 tsp. honey

3 Tbsp. soy sauce

1 Tbsp. sake (optional)

1/4 tsp. dry mustard,
  or 1 tsp. prepared mustard

2 Tbsp. oil

1 medium onion, minced

1 cup cooked brown rice

3 - 4 cloves garlic, minced

1/2 tsp. thyme

1/4 tsp. sage

3 Tbsp. tomato paste

2 oz. walnuts, ground

1 Tbsp. miso

freshly ground pepper

2 additional Tbsp. soy sauce
  (optional)

*This will warm you on a cold winter day. It's also a fun dish to serve because a beautifully sauced head of cabbage is cut open at the table to reveal a "meaty" filling. The tomato sauce is also fat-free, although rich and tasty.*

To core the cabbage, cut out a small cone at the core with a sharp knife. Fill a large pot that will hold the entire head of cabbage half full with water. Bring it to a boil and add the cored cabbage. After the water reboils, simmer the cabbage for about ten minutes. With two forks, start removing the leaves of the cabbage, being careful not to tear them too badly—some tearing is inevitable. They should come off easily. Remove 14 to 16 leaves and set them aside to drain in a colander. Pierce the remaining cabbage (still cooking in water), and if it seems raw or undercooked, boil a few more minutes. If it is tender, remove it and set aside to cool. The cabbage should be tender but still slightly crisp—not mushy. When cool enough to handle, shred or chop it finely. Reserve 1 1/4 cups of the cooking water for later.

Mix the tempeh with the vinegar, honey, soy sauce, sake, and mustard, and sauté it in the oil until lightly browned. Add the minced onion and continue to sauté until tender, about 10 minutes. Add the remaining ingredients including the chopped cabbage, but not the leaves. Season to taste with plenty of freshly ground pepper and the additional two tablespoons of soy sauce, if necessary.

Grease a glass or earthenware round casserole dish and line it with 6 of the outer leaves, allowing the edges to extend beyond the rim of the dish so they can be folded over the top later. Trim the hard rib of the leaves if necessary to make them more pliable. Pack half the tempeh filling into this, then neatly arrange about 4 leaves on top, again cutting away the rib, if desired. Pack the rest of the tempeh mixture in tightly and arrange the remaining leaves over the top ones. Weight down with a heavy plate or lid and cover everything with aluminum foil. Bake at 375° for 1 1/4 hours.

While the cabbage bakes, mix all the ingredients for the sauce and simmer gently, covered, for 30 to 40 minutes. Purée in a blender or food processor, then return to the saucepan and simmer for another 10 minutes, or until thick enough to coat the back of a wooden spoon (boil down if necessary).

To serve, invert the cabbage onto a platter. You should have a shining, glimmering head of cabbage that will look delicious. Pour several tablespoons of the sauce on top, letting it dribble down like frosting on a cake. Cut the cabbage in wedges like a pie and pass the remaining sauce around for individual servings.

*Per serving: Calories: 324, Protein: 15 gm., Fat: 14 gm., Carbohydrates: 31 gm.*

*Tomato Sauce:*

*1 lb. very ripe tomatoes (may substitute canned)*

*1 1/4 cups water from boiling cabbage*

*3/4 cup red wine*

*2 Tbsp. soy sauce*

*2 Tbsp. mirin*

*1/2 Tbsp. honey*

*1/2 Tbsp. miso*

# Curry Stuffed Zucchini Boats

*Serves 4*

2 large, fat zucchini

1 small onion, finely chopped
1 Tbsp. oil
2/3 cup cooked brown rice
1/4 cup raw cashews,
   roughly chopped
1/2 tsp. cumin seeds
1/4 tsp. ground coriander
1/2 tsp. or more curry powder
1 tsp. soy sauce
1/3 cup soy sour cream, page 19
1/3 cup raisins
salt and pepper to taste

*A nice, light curry filling with the crunch of cashews and the sweetness of raisins makes these simple-to-prepare zucchini boats a welcome treat.*

Split the zucchinis in half lengthwise and steam until a fork pierces easily through but they still hold their shape. With a small spoon, scoop out and chop the insides, leaving a wall 1/4" to 1/3" thick. Sauté the onion in the oil until tender and combine with the chopped zucchini pulp and the remaining ingredients. Season to taste and fill the zucchini boats. Bake at 350° for 30 minutes.

*Per serving: Calories: 180, Protein: 5 gm., Fat: 9 gm., Carbohydrates: 20 gm.*

# French Onion Pie

*Over four pounds of onions go into this luscious pie, between layers of flaky filo pastry. The onions get a slow cooking so their sweetness is brought out and no special seasoning or embellishment is necessary. Serve with a salad, some crusty bread, and a crisp, chilled white Zinfandel.*

Heat the oil in a large skillet and sauté the onions in it, covered, for 30 minutes over low heat, stirring occasionally. Then add the 1 tsp. of honey, uncover, and continue cooking for another 20 - 30 minutes. The onions should become brown and very sweet. Season with salt and pepper to taste. You may not be able to add all the onions to the skillet at once; adding them in increments as they cook down during the first 10 minutes is fine. If there is more than a couple of tablespoons of liquid from the onions in the pan, turn the heat up to high and cook a few minutes, uncovered, to evaporate it. This step can be completed several hours or the day before the pie is assembled and baked.

Crumble the tofu and place it in a dry skillet with the salt. Over very low heat, dry-fry the tofu, stirring almost constantly, until it resembles a dry curd cheese, about 15 minutes. Add the soy sauce and cook a moment until it is absorbed.

Assemble the pie for baking. In an oiled pie plate, lay down single layers of filo pastry in a circular fashion, overlapping and brushing melted margarine over each leaf. Keep layering and brushing margarine until half the filo has been used up. Put the tofu in the bottom and place the onions on top. Cover the pie with the remaining filo in a similar fashion and fold the overhanging edges over so as to enclose the pie. Bake in a preheated 350° oven for 35 - 40 minutes until nicely browned. Wait 5 to 10 minutes before cutting and serving.

*Per serving: Calories: 441, Protein: 14 gm., Fat: 24 gm., Carbohydrates: 50 gm.*

*Serves 6-8*

2 Tbsp. oil
4 1/2 lbs. onions, sliced
1 tsp. honey
salt and pepper to taste

1 lb. firm tofu
1 tsp. salt
1 Tbsp. soy sauce

6 - 8 oz. commercial filo dough
  (check the freezer section of
  your supermarket)
4 - 6 oz. margarine, melted

# Chestnut Filled Cabbage Rolls

*Serves 6-8*

*In Japan chestnuts come into season in the fall, and for a brief month the markets are filled with them. Although I have always found cooking and peeling chestnuts to be a chore, I always manage to make these cabbage rolls at least once or twice during chestnut season—they are delicious enough to be worth the trouble. The rich, but fat-free red wine sauce is cooked along with the cabbage rolls, so aside from the task of removing chestnuts from their shells (a job which is greatly expedited by following the instructions below), it is a relatively simple dish to make. I have tried using dried chestnuts in this dish but without good results. Canned or bottled chestnuts, if they have been packed in water and not sugar syrup, can be substituted for the fresh ones successfully and will make the dish a breeze. The filling can be made several days in advance and refrigerated or frozen. Final assembly and cooking should begin two hours before serving.*

*1 1/4 lbs. whole chestnuts,
   or one 14 oz. can or bottle*

*1 medium cabbage*
*1 Tbsp. oil*
*1 medium onion, chopped fine*
*1 cup cooked brown rice*

*2 Tbsp. margarine*
*4 Tbsp. flour*
*1 cup hot soy milk*
*salt and pepper to taste*
*1/2 tsp. whole dill seeds*
*1/2 tsp. ground allspice*
*1/4 tsp. nutmeg*

If using fresh, whole chestnuts, boil them for 20 - 30 minutes and allow to cool enough to handle before removing them from their shells. I find the whole job goes much faster if the flat side of the chestnut is simply sliced off with a small, sharp knife, then the meat scooped out with a small spoon. The chestnuts do not have to come out whole, as they will be chopped up anyway. Remove any inner brown skin that comes out, since it can be bitter. Chop the chestnuts roughly.

If you are using canned or bottled chestnuts, simply drain, rinse, and chop up roughly (some brands are already chopped).

Core the cabbage with a sharp knife, then remove the outer 12 to 16 leaves. Shred the rest of the cabbage and steam or microwave the outer leaves until tender but not overly soft—they should be pliable, not mushy. Heat the oil in a pan and sauté the onion and shredded cabbage until soft and reduced in volume. Place in a bowl with the chopped chestnuts and brown rice.

Make a thick white sauce by melting the margarine in a small saucepan, adding the flour and cooking a minute. Then add the hot soy milk, stirring with a whisk. Cook over low heat, stirring constantly, until very thick. Flavor with salt and pepper. Add this to the cabbage and chestnuts along with the dill seeds, allspice, and nutmeg. Mix well, adjusting the seasonings as necessary (the flavor of the dill will be released during the cooking).

To stuff the cabbage leaves, take one leaf at a time and place it in front of you with the outside of the leaf facing up. With a small, sharp knife slice off the hard rib that forms a bump. Turn the leaf over and place about 1/3 cup of the mixture at the bottom of the leaf, over the rib. Fold the right and left sides over, then roll up tightly. Secure with a toothpick or piece of thread if the rolls won't fit absolutely snug in the pan.

Place the rolls loose side down in a deep frying pan or dutch oven. Mix the ingredients for the red wine sauce together and pour over the rolls. Top with a tight-fitting lid and cook over low heat for 45 to 50 minutes, or until the sauce has been reduced to a thick glaze.

*Per serving: Calories: 258, Protein: 5 gm., Fat: 6 gm., Carbohydrates: 46 gm.*

*Red Wine Sauce:*
*1 1/2 cups good stock*
*1 cup red wine*
*2 Tbsp. soy sauce*
*4 Tbsp. mirin*
*4 Tbsp. tomato paste*
*2 bay leaves*

# French Moussaka

*Serves 6-8*

*Served with Rich Brown Sauce this is a superb creation. Plump little eggplants (the Japanese variety if you can get them) are stuffed with a "meaty" mixture of tofu and walnuts and seasoned delicately with herbs and a hint of cinnamon. It takes a little time to make both the sauce and the dish, but if you make the sauce several days, or even weeks, ahead of time and freeze it, all goes fairly quickly and you and your guests will reap great rewards. For this gourmet dish, get out your best china and adorn each plate as beautifully as you can with a few vegetables to balance the color of the purple eggplants. A delicate mousse or terrine to start the dinner would be nice, followed by a green salad or a light soup. Top it off with Pumpkin Ice Cream, page 213, or the luscious Strawberry Almond Tart, pages 206-7.*

*8 - 12 small eggplants*

*1 medium onion, minced*

*1 - 2 Tbsp. olive oil*

*2 oz. mushrooms, minced*

*4 - 5 fresh or reconstituted shiitake mushrooms, minced*

*1/3 cup Rich Brown Sauce, page 74*

*1 Tbsp. margarine*

*1 Tbsp. flour*

In selecting the eggplants, choose the plumpest ones available. If they are very small, you may want to serve two per person. Wash them and slice in half lengthwise. With a sharp knife make a few deep gashes in the cut side. Sprinkle with salt and let drain, cut side down, in a colander for 20 to 30 minutes. Rinse under cold water and squeeze gently. Bake in a 375° oven for about twenty minutes until soft.

While the eggplants bake, sauté the onions in a tablespoon or two of olive oil until tender. Place the mushrooms and shiitake in a thin cloth and wring out their juices into a bowl (to add to the Brown Sauce later) until the mushrooms are very dry. Add them to the onions and continue sautéing until soft.

If you are preparing the Rich Brown Sauce simultaneously, add the mushroom juices and simmer along with the rest of the ingredients. If the sauce has ben prepared ahead of time, add the mushroom juices while reheating it and allow it to simmer for at least 15 minutes. Remove 1/3 cup of this to thicken so it will bind the filling. Make a roux by melting the margarine and adding the flour, then add the 1/3 cup sauce and cook until very thick, stirring constantly.

When the eggplants are tender and have been allowed to cool slightly, scoop out the pulp with a spoon, leaving the skins and a thin layer of pulp intact. Reserve the skins as they will be stuffed with the mixture.

Add 2/3 of the chopped pulp to the onions and mushrooms and combine with all of the other ingredients except the breadcrumbs, cinnamon, and eggplant skins. Add enough of the breadcrumbs to thicken and hold the filling together and add a dash or two of cinnamon. Season with salt and pepper to taste, adjusting the seasonings as necessary. Fill half the skins with this mixture, mounding it highly, and top with the remaining skins to form "whole" eggplants. Place on a lightly greased cookie sheet and bake for 20 minutes at 350° until the filling looks brown, almost like ground meat.

Pour a generous serving of Rich Brown Sauce on each plate, then position a baked eggplant or two nicely in the center. Surround the eggplants with steamed green beans, asparagus, green peas, or other vegetables, and add a little grilled red bell pepper or tomato for color.

*Per serving: Calories: 340, Protein: 15 gm., Fat: 12 gm., Carbohydrates: 48 gm.*

*12 - 15 oz. firm tofu, frozen, thawed and squeezed dry, and crumbled finely*

*1/3 cup walnuts, finely ground*

*1 - 2 Tbsp. tomato paste*

*1 Tbsp. miso*

*1/2 tsp. thyme*

*1/2 tsp. rosemary*

*1 clove garlic, minced*

*1 - 2 dashes cinnamon*

*1/2 cup or more dry breadcrumbs*

*salt and pepper to taste*

# Herbed Soybean Casserole or Stew

*Serves 4 as a casserole, 4-6 as a stew*

*This rich and delicious concoction will warm you through and through on a cold winter night. The quantity of liquid given here will produce a luscious casserole, but a few extra cups of stock, red wine, and seasonings can be thrown in to extend it and produce a hearty stew that is quite fine to serve an after-theater crowd. If you opt for the stew rather than the casserole, you may cook it on top of the stove instead of the oven. With a salad and some crusty bread it is a meal in itself.*

1 medium onion, chopped

1 large clove garlic, minced

2 Tbsp. olive oil

1 1/2 cups cooked soybeans
   (firm but tender)

1 medium potato, preferably
   waxy, cut into 1/2" cubes

1/3 lb. mushrooms, sliced thick

1 1/2 cups red wine

1 Tbsp. miso

1 Tbsp. tomato paste

1 tsp. salt

1 tsp. marjoram

1 tsp. rosemary

1/2 tsp. ground sage

1/2 cup minced parsley

breadcrumbs for topping
   (optional)

Sauté the onions and garlic in the oil until tender, then mix all the ingredients and place in a casserole dish. Cover and bake at 350° for 1 hour. If desired, remove the cover for the last 10 minutes of baking and top with breadcrumbs. The liquid will have reduced to a nicely flavored sauce and the potatoes and soybeans will be very tender.

*Soybean Stew*: Sauté the onions and garlic in a large dutch oven until tender. Add the remaining ingredients plus an extra half-cup of red wine and about 3 cups of stock. Cover and simmer for 45 minutes to 1 hour. Adjust the seasonings as necessary, adding more miso, tomato paste, etc.

*Per serving: Calories: 278, Protein: 11 gm., Fat: 7 gm., Carbohydrates: 27 gm.*

# Pasta with Creamy Garlic Sauce

*A lot of garlic goes into this velvety, white sauce, but the gentle simmering leaves only a mellow and sweet flavor. Garlic lovers who prefer a more "garlicky" taste can double the amount called for.*

Simmer the peeled garlic in the stock until tender, about 8 minutes, in an uncovered pot over medium-high heat. The liquid should be reduced by 1/3. Purée the garlic and stock in a blender or food processor and add the oil a little at a time while the blender is still running. The more oil you add, the richer the sauce will be; it should be white and have body. Season with salt and pepper and add the parsley. Set aside to reheat before serving.

Prepare the vegetables as desired. Some good choices are lightly steamed broccoli, cauliflower or zucchini, grilled eggplant cubes, mushrooms, cherry tomatoes, or strips of lightly grilled red, yellow, or green bell peppers. Spring and summer vegetables are the best, but, with the exception of broccoli and cauliflower, those of the cabbage family do not go well with the sauce. Use your imagination and whatever looks good in your garden or produce market. Don't over-cook the vegetables; they should remain tender-crisp.

Prepare the pasta to al dente and drain well. You might want to try the Homemade Tofu Pasta on pages 142-3 and cut it into linguine or fettucine—remember that freshly-made pasta cooks in mere moments. Toss with the tablespoon of olive oil and extra minced garlic. Divide into four portions on plates,
arrange vegetables over each serving, and pour the sauce over. Serve immediately.

*Per serving: Calories: 511, Protein: 13 gm., Fat: 19 gm., Carbohydrates: 71 gm.*

*Serves 4*

1 large head garlic, separated and peeled*

2 cups shiitake, wild mushroom, or other good vegetable stock

1/4 - 1/3 cup extra virgin olive oil

salt and pepper to taste

1/2 cup finely chopped parsley

approx. 3 - 4 cups of seasonal vegetables of choice

4 servings of spaghetti, linguine or fettucine

1 Tbsp. olive oil

2 - 4 or more cloves garlic, minced finely or put through a garlic press

*Cloves are easier to peel if immersed in boiling water for 30 seconds.*

# Savory Tempeh and Vegetable Stew

*Serves 6-8*

*1 lb. tempeh*

*Marinade:*
*1 cup red wine*
*1/4 cup soy sauce*
*1 Tbsp. oil*
*1 Tbsp. mirin*
*1/8 tsp. allspice*
*1 Tbsp. nutritional yeast flakes*
*oil for deep frying*

*For the stew:*
*4 Tbsp. oil or margarine*
*2 large onions, sliced or cut into*
   *chunks*
*1/2 cup unbleached white flour*
   *or whole wheat pastry flour*
*1 quart hot stock*

*A deep, rich, flavorful stew that can be part of a grand meal or a simple one accompanied by just salad and bread, and an excellent bottle of red wine.*

The stewed vegetables can be prepared several days in advance and refrigerated or frozen. In that case, prepare the tempeh the day of serving in order to have it as fresh as possible. Several hours or the day before, mix the marinade for the tempeh. Cut the tempeh into 3/4" cubes and marinate for several hours or overnight. Heat oil in a deep fryer or wok and fry the marinated tempeh a few pieces at a time until well-browned and crisp. Drain on absorbent paper. A second frying will produce a crispier surface, but is optional. If you prefer not to fry, the tempeh can be baked in a slow oven (300°) until browned, about 40 minutes—but it may not have the same nutty flavor that many people enjoy.

To make the stew, heat the oil or margarine in a large dutch oven or heavy-bottom pot and sauté the onions, covered, until soft. Add the flour, cook two minutes while stirring constantly over low heat, then add the stock. Cook until slightly thickened, stirring constantly, then add the remaining ingredients except the tempeh. Cover and simmer gently for 45 minutes. Add the tempeh and cook another 25 to 30 minutes. The stew should be extremely rich and flavorful with a slightly thick consistency. Top with minced parsley, if desired.

*Per serving: Calories: 366, Protein: 19 gm., Fat: 14 gm., Carbohydrates: 34 gm.*

*For the stew (cont.):*

6 - 7 dried shiitake mushrooms,
    reconstituted and quartered

1/2 to 3/4 lb. mushrooms,
    quartered or sliced thickly

2 carrots, in 1/4" slices

2 potatoes, preferably waxy, diced

2 large, very ripe tomatoes,
    chopped

1 head garlic, peeled and sliced

3 Tbsp. tomato paste

2 Tbsp. miso

1 1/4 - 1 1/2 cups red wine

1/4 cup soy sauce

3 Tbsp. Rich Yeast Flavoring
    Powder, page 170
    or 2 Tbsp. nutritional yeast

1 tsp. thyme

1 tsp. rosemary

1/2 tsp. sage

1/2 tsp. savory

1/2 tsp. allspice

1/4 tsp. cloves

2 bay leaves

# Vegetable Sesame Tart

*Serves 6-8*

*I created this dish for a department store cooking demonstration in Tokyo where they asked me to design picnic food. It was right around "Hanami" season (literally translated as "blossom viewing" season) when cherry blossoms are in full bloom and the Japanese go to wine and dine under the blanket of pink blossoms. During the season the parks, gardens, and cemeteries (where some of the loveliest blossoms can be found) become unrecognizable with the accumulating garbage from the Bacchanalian revelries. Unfortunately, those who get to the parks late in the season end up seeing more wrappers and bottles than trees, and thus must indulge even more in wine and yummy things like this tart in order to successfully ignore the trash.*

*Vegetable Sesame Tart is a good dish to make for cold buffets or anytime when you want to relax with your guests rather than do last minute things in the kitchen. The crunchy crust made from soy flour, sesame seeds, and wheat germ complements the fresh vegetable filling. Serve with a light, fruity wine like a rose or, better yet, the crisper white Zinfandel.*

*Crust:*

*1 cup minus 2 Tbsp. whole wheat pastry flour*

*1/4 cup wheat germ*

*1/4 cup soy flour*

*1/3 cup hulled white sesame seeds*

*1/2 tsp. salt*

*1/4 cup corn or safflower oil*

*1 tsp. honey*

*4 - 5 Tbsp. water*

To make the crust, mix the flour, wheat germ, soy flour, sesame seeds, and salt. Add the oil while stirring with a fork. Add the honey, stir a few times to mix, and then add the water and combine into a ball. A little more or less water may be required due to the moisture content of the flours. Add enough to hold it together but not too much at a time or you could make a damp mess of things. Press into a deep-dish pie or tart tin and bake for 15 minutes in a 375° oven.

To make the filling, crumble the tofu and place in a skillet with the salt. Stir constantly over low heat until it resembles dry curds—about 15 minutes. Steam the broccoli lightly and sauté the onions and carrots in the oil until tender-crisp. Add the mushrooms to the onions and carrots and cook another minute over medium to high heat to keep the vegetables fairly dry. Flavor with salt, pepper, and a teaspoon of soy sauce. Place the tofu in the pre-baked crust and spread it to cover the bottom evenly. Over that arrange the onions, mushrooms, and carrots, then the broccoli and sliced potatoes. Mix the tahini with the water and the remaining soy sauce to make a thick, creamy sauce and pour over all. Top with the sliced tomatoes and bake for 30 to 40 minutes at 375°. Allow to cool for at least 15 minutes before cutting and serving as it is very crumbly when hot. Serve either warm or at room temperature.

*Per serving: Calories: 355, Protein: 16 gm., Fat: 19 gm., Carbohydrates: 30 gm.*

*Filling:*
*14 - 16 oz. tofu, pressed*
  *(see page 24)*
  *or 8 - 10 oz. pre-pressed, firm*
  *tofu*
*1/2 tsp. salt*
*1 stalk broccoli, broken into small*
  *flowers*
*1 medium onion, sliced*
*1 carrot, sliced thinly*
*1 Tbsp. oil*
*1/4 lb. mushrooms, sliced*
*salt and pepper to taste*
*2 - 3 Tbsp. soy sauce*

*1/3 lb. potatoes, sliced 1/4" thick*
*1/3 cup tahini or sesame paste*
*1/4 cup water*
*1 large tomato, sliced into 1/4"*
  *rings*

# Tofu Bourguignon

*Serves 4-6*

*See photo on page 100.*

*1 lb. frozen tofu, thawed*
*(see page 23)*

*1 1/4 cups red wine*

*5 Tbsp. mirin*

*5 Tbsp. soy sauce*

*2 - 3 Tbsp. miso*

*2 cloves garlic, minced*

*2 Tbsp. red wine*
*or balsamic vinegar*

*1/2 cup unbleached white*
*or whole wheat pastry flour*

*3 Tbsp. oil*

*1 medium onion, finely chopped*

*12 oz. mushrooms, sliced*

*3/4 cup frozen peas*

*approx. 2/3 cup rich soy cream*
*or milk*

*1 - 2 tsp. arrowroot, kuzu,*
*or cornstarch to thicken,*
*if necessary*

*This rich, tasty creation brims with mushrooms and chewy pieces of tofu in an aromatic red wine sauce. It will taste as if it took hours to prepare, although it can be whipped up in less than a half-hour (not including the time needed for marinating the tofu). If possible, make your own fettucine to serve with it. Although best with pasta, it can also be served with brown rice or crusty bread to soak up the delicious sauce. Tempeh can be substituted for the tofu but it cannot duplicate frozen tofu's chewy texture.*

After the tofu has thawed, press gently between both hands to extract as much water as possible without breaking or tearing it. Cut it into squares about 3/8" x 1" x 1 1/4". Mix the red wine, mirin, soy sauce, miso, garlic, and vinegar, and marinate the tofu in this mixture for at least 30 minutes (several hours if desired). Remove the tofu one piece at a time and squeeze lightly to remove some, but not all, of the marinade that it had absorbed. If you press too hard, you will end up with a tasteless piece of tofu; if you don't extract any of the marinade, the tofu may taste too "winey." Measure the remaining marinade after doing this for all the pieces— you should have about 1 1/2 cups. If you have too much, sprinkle some back onto the tofu; if not enough, squeeze the tofu a bit more. Flour the tofu lightly and sauté in 2 Tbsp. oil on both sides until brown and crispy. Remove from the pan and set aside.

Wipe out the skillet with a paper towel and add another tablespoon of oil. Add the chopped onion, cover, and sauté until tender, then add the mushrooms and cover again. Cook over low heat about five minutes until the mushroom juices begin to ooze out. Add the remaining marinade and simmer for another 10 minutes. Add the green peas and cook for another two minutes. Now add the soy milk or cream and cook another minute or two to allow flavors to blend. It should thicken, but if it does not, dissolve a teaspoon or two of arrowroot or kuzu in a little more milk and add to it, stirring constantly, until the sauce has some body. Add the tofu pieces, cook another 3 minutes, then check the flavor, adjusting the seasonings and adding more soy cream, if necessary. Serve immediately over pasta, such as fettucine cooked al dente.

*Tempeh Bourguignon:* Make as for the Tofu Bourguignon recipe, substituting 8 oz. tempeh for the tofu. Marinate for at least 1 hour, then bake the pieces on an oiled sheet for about 20 minutes in a 350° oven or until browned. The rest of the recipe is the same, but the vinegar may be increased to 3 tablespoons, if desired.

*Per serving: Calories: 304, Protein: 13 gm., Fat: 11 gm., Carbohydrates: 35 gm.*

# Oriental Stuffed Eggplant

Serves 3-6

*A very tasty, Japanese-inspired dish. If possible, use the slender, long Japanese eggplants in order to make attractive individual servings. To save time, you can cook them several hours or the day before. Serve with brown rice, miso soup, and some simple sautéed vegetables.*

1/3 lb. tempeh, cut into short
   sticks 1/4" x 3/4"

3 Tbsp. soy sauce

3 Tbsp. water

2 tsp. grated ginger

1 tsp. dark sesame oil

1 Tbsp. rice vinegar

1 Tbsp. oil

3 long or 6 short small eggplants
   (Japanese , if possible)

oil for brushing onto eggplant
   surfaces

5 Tbsp. hulled sesame seeds,
   lightly toasted

1 oz. miso, (1 - 1 1/2 Tbsp.)

2 Tbsp. mirin

1 tsp. grated ginger mixed with
   1 Tbsp. water

Several hours or the day before serving the dish, marinate the tempeh sticks in a mixture consisting of the soy sauce, water, grated ginger, sesame oil, and rice vinegar. After marinating, remove from the marinade and sauté the tempeh in a tablespoon of oil until browned, then add the remaining marinade and continue sautéing until the liquid has been completely absorbed.

Split the eggplants in half lengthwise and brush the cut surfaces lightly with oil. Bake in a 350° oven for ten to fifteen minutes, depending on their size, until tender. When cool enough to handle, scoop out the insides, leaving a thin wall and being careful not to tear the skin. Lightly chop the removed pulp and place in a bowl.

In preparing the sesame seeds it's always preferable to start with untoasted hulled seeds and toast them yourself, since pre-toasted ones quickly become rancid and you won't get the necessary nutty flavor. Place the seeds in a small skillet and cook over low heat, stirring constantly, until you hear them begin to crackle. Remove immediately and do not allow them to color at all; they will puff up slightly. Pound the toasted seeds in a suribachi (a Japanese mortar with grooves; a regular mortar and pestle can be used but takes more effort) until the seeds are finely ground and begin to show a gleam of oil. A food processor or blender can also be used, but be careful that the sesame seeds do not turn into butter or paste; you want to release the oil so that the seeds look slightly sticky but not turn it into tahini. Mix in the miso, mirin, and the additional grated ginger and water mixture. Add the tempeh and eggplant pulp and fold together gently but completely. Fill the eggplant skins and bake for 20 to 25 minutes at 350° until well-browned. They can be served hot, warm, or at room temperature.

*Per serving: Calories: 224, Protein: 8 gm., Fat: 9 gm., Carbohydrates: 27 gm.*

# Homemade Tofu Pasta

*Serves 4-6*

8 oz. tofu

1 Tbsp. oil (optional)

1/2 tsp. salt

2 cups high gluten flour,

    *unbleached white, whole wheat*

    *or a combination*

*(semolina can also be used)*

*Tofu substitutes wonderfully for eggs in this great cholesterol-free homemade pasta. Be sure to use a flour with a high gluten content to get a pasta that will hold up. It is much simpler than it may seem to make your own pasta and the rewards are great.*

Cream the tofu in a blender or food processor and add the oil and salt. If you are using a food processor, the flour can be added directly to the work bowl and processed until mixed. Otherwise, remove the tofu after creaming and mix it with the flour in a separate bowl. Since a pliable dough is desired, start with 1 1/2 cups of flour and add the remaining 1 cup a little at a time to produce an earlobe-consistency that is soft but not sticky. Knead the dough for about 10 minutes until stretchy and very smooth. Allow to rest for 5 minutes before rolling it out.

Flour the rolling surface and roll out the dough 1/16" thick (or twice that if you like thicker pasta). Allow it to dry for 15 minutes before cutting it into the desired shape and length. With a sharp knife cut into lasagne, fettucine, linguine, spaghetti, or whatever you like. If you have a pasta machine, follow the manufacturer's directions for cutting.

Freshly made pasta cooks in 2 to 3 minutes, depending on size and length. After bringing a pot of salted water to boil, add the pasta and cook al dente. Drain and serve *immediately* with the sauce of your choice, as it will cool quickly, softening as it does.

If you are not going to cook the pasta right away, leave it on the surface where it was cut, covered loosely with plastic wrap, or sprinkle with flour and pile neatly on a plate so that the noodles do not stick together.

Another Oriental way to serve homemade pasta is to cook it al dente, drain it, and toss the strands lightly with a little bit of oil, using your fingers to be sure the pasta strands separate. Keep covered until dinner time. Coil the strands in a non-stick frying pan, cover, and warm over low heat. Flip over when lightly browned on the bottom and continue cooking until heated through. Transfer to a platter and top with sauce.

*Per serving: Calories: 245, Protein: 27 gm., Fat: 3 gm., Carbohydrates: 28 gm.*

# Pasta with Three Mushrooms

*Serves 4*

8 oz. each of button, oyster, and
  enoki mushrooms
  (straw mushrooms)
  or other wild mushrooms
  of choice
3 Tbsp. olive oil
3 tsp. or more of garlic, minced
1 cup or more red wine
1/2 tsp. rosemary
1/2 cup parsley, chopped

4 servings of spaghetti, vermicelli
  or linguine

*Here is a simple, flavorful repast.*

This cooks up in less than ten minutes, so start boiling the water for the pasta as you begin to prepare the mushroom sauce.

Slice the button mushrooms and separate the oyster mushrooms and enoki into individual pieces. If you are using larger oyster mushrooms, tear them into bite-size pieces. Heat the olive oil in a skillet and sauté the mushrooms with the garlic for two to three minutes. Add the wine and rosemary and cook five minutes. Add the parsley and cook another minute or two. Season to taste with salt and pepper.

Cook the pasta to al dente. Drain well, toss with a little olive oil and salt and top with sauce. Serve immediately.

*Per serving: Calories: 492, Protein: 14 gm., Fat: 10 gm., Carbohydrates: 74 gm.*

# Ginger Tempeh with Green Peppers

*A simple and tasty Chinese-style tempeh dish. Serve with brown rice and another dish of steamed or stir-fried veggies.*

Combine the shiitake stock, soy sauce, and mirin in a saucepan with a tight fitting lid. Add the tempeh, cover, and simmer for 15 minutes until at least 3/4 of the liquid is gone. Remove the tempeh from the broth, saving the remainder of the broth for a later step. Heat the oil in a wok or frying pan and sauté the tempeh over high heat until browned. Remove the tempeh from the pan, wipe out, add a bit more oil and quickly sauté the green peppers. Add the tempeh and the chopped green onions, sauté one minute, then add the remaining broth and continue cooking another minute or two until most of it is absorbed. If you like, you may thicken the broth in the pan with a little arrowroot or kuzu to make a glazed sauce.

*Per serving: Calories: 264, Protein: 12 gm., Fat: 16 gm., Carbohydrates: 16 gm.*

*Serves 4*

1 1/4 cups shiitake stock
   *(from reconstituted shiitake)*

*3 Tbsp. soy sauce*

*3 Tbsp. mirin*

*8 oz. tempeh, cut into 1" sticks*

*oil for sautéing*

*8 oz. green bell peppers, slivered*

*1 bunch green onions or scallions,
   chopped*

*2 - 3 tsp. freshly grated ginger*

# Gâteau de Crêpes

*See photo on page 149.*

*Serves 6 -8*

*Literally a "cake of crêpes," this epicurean delight looks like a colorful Provençal painting; thin pancakes alternate with green, brown, and red and white fillings, and the whole concoction is frosted with a chunky tomato sauce (Fresh Tomato Sauce, page 78). In both flavor and appearance, this will definitely be the pièce de resistance of any menu. For the crêpes themselves I give a recipe without eggs for vegans. When pressed for time you could even use store-bought flour tortillas.*

*Eggless Crêpes:*

*2 Tbsp. egg replacer*

*1 1/2 cups water*

*1 cup soy milk*

*1 tsp. salt*

*4 Tbsp. oil*

*2 cups flour (whole wheat pastry, unbleached white, or a mixture)*

*1/2 cup garbanzo (chick pea) flour (available in natural or Middle Eastern food stores)*

*Making the Crêpes:* The crêpes can be made days, even weeks ahead and frozen, and the fillings and sauce made the day before, leaving only the simple assembly and baking for the day you are to serve it. This organization makes the recipe far less complicated and time-consuming than it may first appear. You may have a good half-dozen or more crêpes left over, so wrap and freeze them for later use in something like Wild Rice Crêpes with Nutty Almond Sauce, page 114.

Place the egg replacer with 1/2 cup water in blender and blend until smooth. Add the remaining ingredients and blend for 1 minute at high speed. These can be cooked right away.

*For the Gâteau, have ready:*

*7 crêpes*

*1 recipe Fresh Tomato Sauce, page 78*

To cook the crêpes, the choice of skillet you use is important. Use either a well-seasoned omelette or crêpe pan, or a non-stick skillet (with an 8" bottom). Place it over a low flame and brush it lightly with oil; you will only need to oil it once for the whole batch. Let it heat for a few moments, then TAKE THE PAN OFF THE HEAT, pour in about 3 or 4 tablespoons of batter and tilt the pan all around so that the batter coats the bottom of the pan lightly. If you have extra batter, pour it back into the bowl before returning the pan to the stove. Put the pan back on the burner and cook for a few minutes over a gentle flame until lightly browned, and then flip over and cook the other side. The second side will not take as long to brown. Repeat the procedure until all the batter is used up, stacking the crêpes. They can be used immediately or wrapped well and refrigerated or frozen.

For the first filling, cut the eggplants in half and make several gashes with a sharp knife into the flesh of the cut side. Brush the surfaces lightly with olive oil, and bake at 350° for about 30 to 40 minutes, until very soft. When cool enough to handle, scoop out the flesh with a spoon and chop well. Mix with the walnuts and garlic and salt to taste. Set aside.

For the second filling, sprinkle the grated zucchini with the teaspoon of salt and set in a colander to drain for 15 minutes. At the end of the 15 minutes squeeze the zucchini to rid them of most of their juice (this juice can be saved for use in soup stock). Wash the spinach well, dry, and chop roughly. Heat the olive oil in a large skillet, and sauté the zucchini with the garlic for 3 to 4 minutes over medium heat, then add the spinach and cook until wilted and the vegetables are tender-crisp. There should be very little liquid in the pan. Set aside.

For the third filling, cut the peppers in half and remove the tops and seeds. Broil the outsides of the peppers until charred, then peel the skins off. Dice into small pieces. Mash the tofu very well (an electric mixer can be used) and mix with the peppers and lemon juice. Add salt and plenty of black pepper to taste.

*Filling 1:*
*2 large eggplants (1 1/2 lbs.)*
*2 cloves garlic, minced*
*1/2 cup walnuts, ground*
*salt to taste*

*Filling 2:*
*1 Tbsp. olive oil*
*1 1/2 lbs. zucchini, grated*
*1 tsp. salt*
*1 bunch spinach, washed and*
   *trimmed*
*1 - 2 cloves garlic*
*4 oz. soy cheese, mozarella or*
   *garlic-herb (optional)*

*Filling 3:*
*8 oz. firm tofu*
*1 lb. red bell peppers*
*2 Tbsp. lemon juice*
*salt and freshly ground pepper to*
   *taste*

*(continued on next page)*

*(Gâteau de Crêpes, continued)*

To assemble the Gâteau, lightly oil a round baking dish or oven-proof platter a little larger than the crêpes. Place one crêpe in the dish and spread one-half of the first filling on it. Place another crêpe on top and spread one-half of the second filling on it. Sprinkle on half of the optional cheese, if desired. Top with another crêpe and spread half the third filling. Repeat the procedure once more, topping it with a nice looking crêpe—torn ones can be used for the lower layers. Spread 1/2 cup of the Fresh Tomato Sauce on top and bake for 1 hour at 350°.

Allow to cool for 10 minutes before cutting. With a sharp knife cut in wedges like a pie and serve with additional Fresh Tomato Sauce.

This is also very tasty cold the next day.

*Per serving: Calories: 366, Protein: 14 gm., Fat: 17 gm., Carbohydrates: 41 gm.*

# Homemade Gluten

*Makes almost 4 cups raw gluten*

*Let me introduce you to seitan and other highly metamorphic concoctions! Homemade gluten has so many uses and can transform into such a variety of textures and flavors that it is really worth spending two or three hours once or twice a month to make a big batch to have on hand in either the refrigerator or freezer. It is also a great deal of fun to make and always surprising the first time to see plain, whole wheat flour suddenly metamorphose into a stretchy, gum-like substance, which again transforms into myriad "meaty" textures. Bascially gluten is wheat protein and is isolated by first mixing water and flour together to make a dough, then washing away the starch and bran. Raw gluten can be baked, fried, stewed, or boiled, and will come to resemble ground meat, turkey, roasts, etc. If flavored properly, it is delicious and will surprise your guests.*

*The Chinese have used gluten in vegetarian cooking for centuries. In the United States, gluten is most commonly found in the form of "seitan," where gluten is stewed with soy sauce and stock until it becomes a dark, rich, chewy substance. Try the variety of recipes in this book for gluten, such as Tempeh and Gluten Burgers, page 157, Pâté en Croûte, pages 42-3, and the absolutely amazing Great Gluten Turkey, pages 158-9. And have fun! You will feel like a magician with gluten.*

*Basic Raw Gluten:*  The recipe here is for about 3 pounds of flour, but if your bowl will hold more, make more since the work is all the same. The important point to remember is to use a high-gluten whole wheat flour. Whole wheat pastry flour will not give you the same results. If you're in doubt, ask for the best flour for breadbaking—it has the highest gluten content.

*3 lbs. or more high-gluten whole wheat flour*
*3 cups or more water*

Place the flour in a large bowl and add the water while stirring constantly. Add enough water to make a very firm dough—it should be much firmer than bread dough. Allow this to sit for at least 1 hour. No kneading or setting overnight is necessary.

Place the bowl containing the dough in the sink. Fill it with tap water and begin to massage the dough. The water will grow very white and milky at first as the starch rinses out. This liquid can be saved and used in place of arrowroot or

*Great Gluten Turkey with Dressing, pgs. 158-160,  Gluten Gravy, pg. 161,  and Orange Maple Yams, pg. 196*

cornstarch to thicken sauces and such. It will keep for about two weeks in the refrigerator. It you don't save it, discard the water as it gets cloudy and fill the bowl with fresh water. Keep filling with fresh water, massaging the dough and discarding the water for about ten to fifteen minutes until the water grows gradually clear. During this process as the starch and bran get washed away, the dough will shrink in size and at one point may appear to be falling apart completely. In the end it will all congeal into one stretchy mass. When it looks like you have a giant wad of well-chewed bubble gum, you have transformed flour into raw gluten. You can now prepare it into a number of delectable substances.

Although a bowl is all that is really necessary to produce raw gluten, a plastic or steel colander (not wire mesh) can be a great help, especially at the stage when the gluten feels as if it is disintegrating. The water can be poured off through the colander and the colander will catch any loose bits of gluten.

*How To Use Vital Wheat (Instant) Gluten Flour:* If you don't mind skipping the magic show of transforming wheat flour into gluten, you can greatly expedite the process by simply using instant gluten flour (vital wheat gluten). All you need to do is mix with water, and voila! Instant raw gluten appears. Actually, there is even an advantage here, since seasonings and flavorings can be mixed right into the flour with the water, yielding a tastier product. (Instant gluten flour is available in natural food stores or by mail order, see page 245).

To make raw gluten from instant gluten flour, simply combine the flour with the water. Mix well. Part of the water may be replaced by stock, soy sauce, miso, tomato paste, liquid aminos or another liquid flavoring agent. Various herbs, spices and other seasonings can be added to the liquid before you add it to the flour.

*2 1/2 cups instant gluten flour*
*2 cups water*

# Basic Ground Gluten

*This can be used either alone or in combination with tempeh to produce chewy sausages, burgers, etc. It will keep 1 week to 10 days refrigerated or can be frozen for longer periods.*

Stretch out Basic Raw Gluten into a circular shape approximately 1/2" thick. Place on a well-greased cookie sheet. Bake in a pre-heated 350° oven for about 30 minutes or until puffed up and golden brown. Pierce with a sharp knife in several places and allow to sit in the oven for another 15 minutes with the oven turned off to allow steam to escape. If you are pressed for time, you can pierce it the last ten minutes of baking. Remove from the oven and cover with a damp cloth until cool. Tear it into chunks and grind in a food processor.

*Per cup: Calories: 349, Protein: 38 gm., Fat: 2 gm., Carbohydrates: 44 gm.*

*Makes 5-6 cups*

*1 recipe Basic Raw Gluten,
   pages 151-2*

# Oven Roasted Gluten

*Makes 6-8 servings*

*Stewing gluten in an oven will produce a firm, chewy texture. The process alone is given below; the liquid used can be anything from plain stock to stock with wine, soy sauce, garlic, wild mushrooms, herbs, etc.*

*1 recipe Basic Raw Gluten, pages 151-2*

Place Basic Raw Gluten in a dutch oven or deep casserole dish. Pour enough stock to fill the pot or dish nearly to the brim. Cover and bake in a 300° oven for 1 1/2 to 2 hours. The gluten will expand and become firm and springy to the touch. The resulting liquid will be very tasty and can be used in sauces or soups. The gluten itself can be sliced, sauced, and served, or can be sautéed or added to stir-fries, etc.

*Per serving:  Calories: 299, Protein: 33 gm.; Fat: 2 gm., Carbohydrates: 37 gm.*

# Stove-Top Gluten

*Stewing gluten on top of the stove will result in a softer, spongier texture than oven-stewed. However, it will firm up in the refrigerator and can be used for sandwiches, etc. Again, it can be flavored a number of different ways by varying the amounts of stock, soy sauce, water, garlic, onions, etc.*

Sauté the onions in the oil in a large dutch oven or pot. Meanwhile, form the raw gluten into a fat log and cut into 1/4" slices. Place the slices in the pot and add water or stock to fill the pot three-quarters of the way. Add desired amounts of the remaining ingredients to flavor the stock. Other vegetables such as celery and carrots may also be added. Cover the pot and stew gently for 1 to 2 hours. The slices will swell and become spongy and chewy, and the liquid will grow quite flavorful.

The slices can be breaded and sauteed, deep-fried, or refrigerated to use in sandwiches. Use the liquid to make soups and sauces.

*Per serving: Calories: 349, Protein: 33 gm., Fat: 6 gm., Carbohydrates: 41 gm.*

*Makes 6-8 servings*

*1 recipe Basic Raw Gluten,*
*    pages 151-2*
*1 - 2 medium onions, sliced*
*2 Tbsp. oil*
*soy sauce*
*garlic*
*herbs*
*nutritional yeast*
*red wine*
*shiitake*

# Deep-Fried Gluten Balls

*Makes 6-8 servings*

*Oil for deep-frying*
*1 recipe Basic Raw Gluten,*
*    pages 151-2*

*This is a favorite Chinese method of preparing gluten. It results in chewy, spongy balls that soak up whatever flavorings they are cooked with.*

Heat the oil for frying. Tear off little 1/2" pieces of raw gluten. Fry until puffed up and browned. Drain and rinse with boiling water to remove excess oil. Allow to cool slightly, then remove the water by squeezing gently. These balls can now be marinated, stir-fried, or stewed as desired.

*Per serving: Calories: 441, Protein: 33 gm., Fat: 18 gm., Carbohydrates: 37 gm.*

# Tempeh and Gluten Burgers

*Homemade ground gluten and tempeh work excellently together to form juicy, chewy, light, and tasty burgers. This is very simple if you have the ground gluten (which can be stored frozen) on hand.*

Mix all the ingredients together, form into patties and sauté on both sides until browned. Serve them on a whole wheat bun or with a sauce.

*Per serving: Calories: 222, Protein: 20 gm., Fat: 5 gm., Carbohydrates: 19 gm.*

*Serves 6-8*

2 cups tempeh, steamed and
   crumbled
2 1/2 to 2 3/4 cups Basic Ground
   Gluten, page 153
1 - 2 cloves garlic, minced
1/2 large onion, fine chopped
2 Tbsp. Rich Nutritional Yeast
   Flavoring, page 170
   or nutritional yeast with
   a 1/2 tsp. each of basil, thyme
   and oregano
3 Tbsp. tomato paste
2 Tbsp. soy sauce
3 Tbsp. peanut butter
1/8 tsp. allspice

# The Great Gluten Turkey

*Serves 8-12*

*See photo on page 150.*

*Using wheat flour:*
10 lbs. high-protein whole wheat
    flour, preferable finely ground
Approximately 14 cups water
1/3 cup Light Nutritional Yeast
    Flavoring, page 171, (or more)

*Using vital wheat gluten flour:*
8 cups vital wheat gluten flour
    mixed with 6 cups water and
    1/2 cup Light Nutritional
    Yeast Flavoring, page 171

One yard of cheesecloth
2/3 cup Light Nutritional Yeast
    Flavoring, page 171, (or more)

*Amazing, fun, incredible, and tasty, this creation will delight and satisfy any vegetarian wondering what to make for the centerpiece of a Thanksgiving or Christmas table. Like any good turkey, this one looks quite imposing with its golden and juicy-looking "skin" which, when cut, reveals white "meat" enclosing whatever kind of dressing you like. Accompanied by a tasty gravy and homemade cranberry sauce, no vegetarian will ever feel left out when the holidays roll around. To complete the meal, try Orange-Maple Yams, page 196, Garlic Rice, page 195, and a crisp green salad.*

*The skin for the turkey is made from "yuba," a product made from the skin that forms when soy milk is heated. It can be purchased as fragile, dry sheets at Japanese food stores, or at certain Chinese markets in the freezer section. "Yuba" is a Japanese term and will not be understood at a Chinese grocery. The Chinese form, often labelled "bean curd sheet" or "bean curd skin," is usually less fragile than the Japanese variety, easier to use and less expensive. To be sure you purchase the right product, avoid flat square sheets which, when closely examined, look like thick canvas (you can actually see the "weave"). Instead buy sheets that look heavily wrinkled. Sometimes they are sold as large (over 20") circles that are folded and sold in small packets. They will be yellow in color. Some tofu cookbooks contain a recipe for making homemade yuba. The process is not hard and can be adopted when commercial yuba is not available.*

The "yuba" must be soaked and reconstituted to a soft, pliable texture before using. It is best to put individual sheets between wet towels until they turn soft and white in color. They are then ready to use.

Using either wheat flour or vital wheat gluten flour, make gluten according to the recipes on pages 151-2. Roll it out into a rectangle approximately 15 inches long and 8 to 10 inches wide. Sprinkle with 1/3 cup yeast flavoring (unless you've added it in with your vital wheat gluten). Roll it up lengthwise. Spread out the cheesecloth and place the gluten roll in the middle. Wrap the sides of the cloth around the gluten roll first, then tie the ends together. It should be wrapped fairly loosely so that the gluten can expand a little while cooking but not so loose that it expands too much and becomes too soft and spongy in texture.

Place the roll in a large pot. Pour over it the gallon of water and the remaining 2/3 cup yeast flavoring. Cover, bring to a boil, turn down the heat, and simmer for 1 1/2 hours. This process can be done up to two days before serving.

Prepare the dressing below or stuffing of your choice. Remove the gluten roll from the stock, saving the stock for gravy. Untie and remove the cheesecloth. Unroll the "turkey" and fill it with the stuffing, or mound the stuffing on a large, greased baking sheet and place the gluten around it. Place the stuffed gluten on a large, greased baking sheet.

Reconstitute the yuba by soaking for five minutes in water in a flat, shallow dish, or between layers of wet towels. It will turn white and be pliable but will still be fragile. Cover the "turkey" with two to three layers of yuba. Melt the margarine and brush the entire "turkey" with some of it. Pour the wine into the remaining margarine: this will be used to baste the "turkey" while baking. If desired, two tablespoons of the yeast flavoring can be added to the margarine-wine mixture to give it an even more authentic flavor.

Place the "turkey" in a preheated 350° oven and bake for 1 1/4 to 1 1/2 hours, basting every 15 minutes with the wine-margarine mixture and the juices in the pan. If it browns too much, cover loosely with aluminum foil.

Carve as you would a regular roast and accompany with stuffing.

*Per serving: Calories: 514, Protein: 46 gm., Fat: 8 gm., Carbohydrates: 58 gm.*

*1 gallon of water*
*1/3 cup margarine*
*1/3 cup white wine*

*2 round circles Chinese bean curd sheet (yuba), or enough smaller squares to cover "turkey" in two or three layers (3 or 4 packets)*

*6 - 8 cups Great Gluten Dressing or stuffing of choice (bread, wild rice, chestnut, etc.)*

# Great Gluten Dressing

*Serves 8-12*

*See photo on page 150.*

*2 Tbsp. margarine*

*1 large onion, chopped*

*2 stalks celery, chopped*

*6 oz. mushrooms, sliced*


*1 1/2 lbs. bread crumbs*

*1 1/2 tsp. sage*

*1 1/2 tsp. marjoram*

*1 1/2 tsp. thyme*

*1 tsp. salt*

*1 cup stock*

Melt the margarine. Sauté the onions, celery, and mushrooms. Combine with the remaining ingredients, moistening with stock as necessary.

*Per serving: Calories: 174, Protein: 7 gm., Fat: 2 gm., Carbohydrates: 30 gm.*

# Gravy for Mock Turkey

Melt the margarine in a saucepan. Add the flour and cook for two minutes. Add the reserved gluten stock, white wine, and soy sauce. Cook, stirring constantly, until thick. For more flavor, an additional tablespoon of the Light Yeast Flavoring may be added.

*Per 1/4 cup serving: Calories: 69, Protein: 0 gm., Fat: 6 gm., Carbohydrates: 4 gm.*

*Makes 1 cup*

*See photo on page 150.*

*2 Tbsp. margarine*
*2 1/2 Tbsp. flour*
*1 cup reserved gluten stock*
*1 Tbsp. white wine*
*several dashes soy sauce*
*1 Tbsp. Light Nutritional Yeast*
*    Flavoring, page 171 (optional)*

# Vegetable Tempura

*Serves 4-6*

*Various vegetables of choice:*

*thinly sliced onions*

*whole or halved mushrooms*

*broccoli flowers*

*zucchini sliced diagonally 1/3"*
 *thick*

*slices of sweet potato*

*slices of kabocha*
 *(Japanese pumpkin)*

*parsley*

*shiitake*

*slices of eggplant*

*string beans*

*asparagus spears*

*very thin carrot sticks*
 *(almost slivers).*

*This famous and wonderful Japanese dish, like sushi, is so highly regarded by the Japanese that people rarely make it at home, leaving it to highly skilled chefs at tempura restaurants. Very good tempura can be expensive, too, but so delicate, light, and tasty that one finds it difficult to believe that it is just vegetables with batter. In no way does it taste like onion rings.*

Tempura is a perfect balance of vegetables coated with just the right amount of batter and deep-fried to a light, crispy perfection. It is then dipped in a soy-based sauce and eaten together with rice. Altogether, it can be a heavenly experience. On the other hand, bad tempura will usually have more batter than the star ingredient inside and be oily and soggy. It is all in the technique of preparation and cooking, and can be duplicated at home. The three important points to remember are:

1. Mix the batter ever so lightly
2. Have the oil at the proper temperature.
3. Never crowd the fryer.

Have all your ingredients ready before you begin frying so that you can dip, fry, and drain quickly and systematically. For deep-frying refined oils usually work best. *Never* re-use frying oil as it not only imparts an unpleasant flavor but is unhealthy.

Wash and drain or dry vegetables and cut them into sizes that can be eaten in two to three bites. Onions and carrots are usually combined with the last of the batter and fried in clumps, so save them for last. Have all the vegetables ready for dipping and frying.

Start heating the oil. Mix the flour, baking soda, and water gently, leaving in some of the lumps and making sure that you do not overmix it. Test the oil for frying—a small drop of batter dropped in should sink and rise to the surface fairly quickly (around 350°). If the batter sinks and does not rise, or rises very slowly, the oil is not hot enough. If it hardly sinks before sizzling at the surface, the oil is too hot. Dip the vegetables in the batter one piece at a time and fry immediately. Do not fry any more vegetables at one time than will cover half the surface of the oil or the temperature of the oil may drop and you will end up with soggy pieces of tempura. Fry until golden brown, about 1 to 2 minutes. Remove and drain, and continue with the remaining vegetables, mixing up more batter if necessary. Onion slices and thin carrot sticks can be combined with the last of the batter and be fried in clumps.

While the vegetables are frying, combine the stock, soy sauce, and mirin, and heat until boiling. Turn down the heat and simmer gently for 2 or 3 minutes.

To serve, pour about a third of a cup of the Tempura Sauce in individual bowls. A little grated ginger or daikon may be added at this time if desired—remove excess water first by wringing with hands. Dip tempura vegetables in the sauce and enjoy with rice.

*Per serving: Calories: 255, Protein: 5 gm., Fat: 11 gm., Carbohydrates: 34 gm.*

*Tempura Tofu:* Serve this with the *Vegetable Tempura* to add contrast, texture, and protein. Slice 1 lb. of frozen tofu that has been thawed and squeezed (see page 23) into pieces approximately 2" x 1" x 1/3". Mix 1/3 cup shiitake stock, 2 Tbsp. mirin, 2 Tbsp. miso, 1 1/2 Tbsp. peanut butter, 3 Tbsp. tomato paste, and 3 Tbsp. soy sauce until smooth. Mix with the tofu and gently squeeze the marinade into the tofu pieces. Dip the tofu pieces in the tempura batter and fry as in the preceding recipe.

*Batter:*
*1 cup whole wheat pastry flour*
   *or unbleached white flour*
*a pinch of baking soda*
*1 cup ice water*

*Tempura Sauce:*
*1 1/2 cups shiitake or konbu stock*
*1/2 - 2/3 cup soy sauce*
*1/4 cup mirin*
*grated ginger root*
   *and/or grated daikon (Japanese*
   *long radish), optional*

*Oil for deep-frying—salad oil*
   *used alone or in combination*
   *with sesame oil*

# Marinated Tofu

*Serves 6*

1 1/2 lbs. pre-pressed tofu
   or 2 lbs. tofu, pressed
   (see page 24)

*Marinade:*
1 cup red wine
1/2 cup soy sauce
2 Tbsp. red wine or balsamic
   vinegar
1/4 cup
3 - 4 cloves garlic, pressed or
   finely minced
3 Tbsp. tomato paste
1 tsp. rosemary
freshly ground pepper

1 Tbsp. olive oil

*Quite succulent and tasty. It can be sautéed or baked, or baked first, then sautéed for those who like their tofu chewy.*

Mix the ingredients for the marinade and place in a large, shallow baking dish or container. Slice the tofu at least 1/4" to 1/3" thick and marinate for at least eight hours (in hot weather don't let it sit out for longer than 24 hours). You may marinate it as long as you like in the refrigerator—three or four days will result in a deep, rich flavor, but shorter periods will still give you a delicious dish.

Sauté the marinated tofu in 1 Tbsp. olive oil on both sides until browned, then add several tablespoons of the remaining marinade and sizzle for a moment. Serve immediately. Or you may first bake the slices on a greased cookie sheet at 350° for thirty minutes. Serve as is with a little marinade, or sauté quickly and serve with the extra marinade. Baked tofu is quite chewy, while simply sautéing it will render a tender, succulent tofu.

*Per serving: Calories: 182, Protein: 12 gm., Fat: 12 gm., Carbohydrates: 6 gm.*

# Smoky Marinated Tofu

*Use the following marinade for a smoky flavor.*

Mix, marinate, and prepare as in the Marinated Tofu recipe on the previous page.

*Per serving: Calories: 188, Protein: 12 gm., Fat: 12 gm., Carbohydrates: 9 gm.*

*Serves 6*

1 1/2 lbs. pre-pressed tofu
  or 2 lbs. tofu, pressed
  (see page 24)

*Marinade:*
1 cup red wine
1/3 cup tomato paste
2 Tbsp. red wine vinegar
2 Tbsp. olive oil
2 Tbsp. sesame oil
3 Tbsp. honey
1 Tbsp. molasses (optional)
1/2 cup soy sauce
3 - 4 cloves garlic, pressed
  or minced
  or 1 tsp. garlic powder
1/2 tsp. cayenne pepper (optional)
2 Tbsp. liquid smoke

1 Tbsp. olive oil

# Believable Bacon

Serves 10

This is the only vegetarian "bacon" I have found to be really satisfying—crispy, chewy, with a smoky flavor. And with no cholesterol, it's the perfect complement to any breakfast, or make yourself a great BLT with it. A delicious, homey Beans and "Bacon" Casserole follows.

8 oz. pre-pressed or firm tofu
(see page 24)

3 Tbsp. good tasting nutritional
yeast

3 Tbsp. soy sauce

Approximately 1 tsp. liquid
smoke flavor

1 Tbsp. oil + non-fat cooking
spray
or 2 - 3 Tbsp. oil

Slice the tofu into pieces 1/8" thick and about the width of a slice of bacon. Spray a skillet (preferably non-stick) with non-fat cooking spray, heat the tablespoon of oil, and cook the tofu slices over a medium-low flame until golden brown and crispy on one side. Flip and cook the other side until browned. The tofu should be crispy. Sprinkle with the nutritional yeast, then add the soy sauce and liquid smoke and stir quickly to coat the tofu slices evenly. Cook for another moment, then serve.

Per serving: Calories: 47, Protein: 3 gm., Fat: 3 gm., Carbohydrates: 2 gm.

# Beans and "Bacon" Casserole

Serves 6

*Simple to make, this tasty, homey casserole will comfort you on winter nights. Serve with Dilly Cabbage, Orange-Maple Yams or Minted Carrots, and some warm rolls.*

Preheat the oven to 350°.

Prepare the "bacon" and set aside. Combine all the other ingredients (the onions and mushrooms do not need to be precooked) and pour into a shallow, rectangular pyrex dish or casserole. Lay the "bacon" strips on top and cover all with aluminum foil. Bake for about 1 hour. There should be a nicely flavored sauce bubbling away. Serve while hot.

*Per serving: Calories: 251, Protein: 15 gm., Fat: 7 gm., Carbohydrates: 28 gm.*

1 - 2 recipes Believable "Bacon"

2 (15 oz.) cans kidney beans
   or 1 large can, with approx.
   1/2 its liquid

1 1/2 onions, chopped

6 - 8 oz. mushrooms, sliced

4 - 6 cloves garlic, minced

1/2 cup red wine

4 - 6 Tbsp. soy sauce

2 Tbsp. flour

# Jeff's Favorite "Neat" Loaf

*Serves 6*

1 large onion, chopped

2 stalks celery, chopped

1 (15 oz.) can garbanzo beans
   (chick peas), drained and
   mashed well

1/2 cup walnuts, ground

1/3 cup wheat germ

1 lb. frozen tofu, defrosted,
   squeezed dry and crumbled
   (see page 23)

2 Tbsp. tomato paste

2 Tbsp. miso

1 - 2 Tbsp. soy sauce

1/2 tsp. allspice

1 tsp. thyme

1/2 tsp. chervil

1 tsp. oregano

freshly ground pepper to taste

3 - 4 Tbsp. tahini mixed with a
   little water to make a thick
   paste

*Topping:*

1/3 cup ketchup

2 Tbsp. soy sauce

*Quite convincing; a great homestyle dish to serve skeptics of tofu and other natural goodies. Serve with ketchup mixed with soy sauce or a tasty gravy.*

Preheat the oven to 350°. Sauté the onions and celery in a little oil or water until tender. Combine all the ingredients and pat into a greased loaf pan. Combine the ingredients for the topping and smear on top of the loaf. Bake for 1 hour. Turn off the heat and allow to sit in the oven for an additional 20 to 30 minutes, or at room temperature for 15 minutes before unmolding and slicing, or it may not hold together well.

Serve with additional topping mix, the following fat-free gravy, or the Gluten Gravy recipe on page 161, using the Rich Nutritional Yeast Flavoring on page 170 instead of the Light Flavoring.

*Per serving: Calories: 374, Protein: 20 gm., Fat: 13 gm., Carbohydrates: 47 gm.*

# Fat-Free Gravy

Makes 1 1/4 cups

Combine all ingredients except the cornstarch mixture and bring to a simmer for 5 minutes. Add the cornstarch mixture a little at a time, stirring constantly until thickened.

*Per 1/4 cup serving: Calories: 47, Protein: 1 gm., Fat: 0 gm., Carbohydrates: 9 gm.*

1 cup water or stock

2 Tbsp. miso

2 Tbsp. soy sauce

1/2 tsp. celery seeds

2 - 3 Tbsp. nutritional yeast
  (or Rich Nutritional Yeast
  Flavoring, page 170)

freshly ground pepper to taste

3 Tbsp. cornstarch mixed with
  enough water to dissolve

# Rich Yeast Flavoring Powder

*This is similar to a beef stock flavoring.*

1 cup good tasting nutritional
    yeast flakes

3 Tbsp. dried parsley

2 Tbsp. salt

1 1/2 Tbsp. dill seeds

1 1/2 Tbsp. onion powder

1 1/2 Tbsp. basil

1 1/2 Tbsp. celery seeds

1 Tbsp. thyme

2 tsp. rosemary

1 Tbsp. black pepper

Combine all ingredients in a blender and pulverize to a powder. Store in a jar in a cool place. Add to soups, loaves, burgers, and to recipes in this book where noted.

# Light Yeast Flavoring Powder

*This has a poultry-type flavor.*

Pulverize all ingredients in a blender until powdered. Store in a jar in a cool place.

1 cup good tasting nutritional
    yeast flakes
1 Tbsp. salt
1/2 tsp. ginger
1/2 tsp. turmeric
1 tsp. black pepper
1 tsp. marjoram
1 tsp. tarragon
1 tsp. paprika
1 tsp. rosemary
2 tsp. sage
2 tsp. celery seed
2 tsp. thyme
2 tsp. garlic powder
2 tsp. onion powder

# *Vegetable Dishes & Salads*

Vegetables are so versatile they can either be the center attraction of a meal or play a delicious supporting role. Whether you opt for a crisp salad or plate of steamed vegetables, here is an opportunity to be as creative as you please and be assured of positive results.

# The Green Salad

avocados

broccoli or cauliflower, very
   slightly steamed (or raw, if
   you like)

capers

carrot curls, thin slices or sticks,
   or grated

cucumbers

fresh herbs—basil, tarragon,
   coriander

jicama (a Mexican root vegetable
   with a sweet taste

mushrooms

olives, oil-cured or Kalamata

red onion slices

pecans or walnuts, toasted

cold potato slices, cooked or
   soaked for several hours to
   remove starch

scallions

sprouts—alfalfa, clover, etc.

string beans, steamed and chilled

sweet red bell peppers

sunflower seeds (raw)

tomatoes—cherry, plum, regular,
   or marinated sun-dried

watercress

Those who live in the United States and can get or make a good salad are lucky. In many countries, salad amounts to no more than a few pieces of tired-looking lettuce with gooey dressing on top. In Japan, the salad that comes with your meals at restaurants is often made of tired looking shredded cabbage with Italian dressing.

Salad is practically a religion in America with everyone following his own sect. Since so many people have such strong feelings about what they want and what they don't want in their salad, I will only attempt to make few suggestions on how to assure that any salad comes out tasting fresh, crisp, and delicious.

If possible, use a variety of lettuce. Iceburg is the least nutritious and tasty, and unless you are really partial to it, should play second fiddle (or no fiddle at all) to the many other greens available. Lettuce such as romaine, red leaf, escarole, butterhead or boston, and tender spinach leaves, etc., all lend a variety of tastes and textures to your salad. Of course, you may choose to use just one or two of the greens.

Whatever you do, the greens must be CRISP. To bring back life to tired-looking greens, soak them in a bowl of very cold water for fifteen minutes. Drain, and pat each leaf gently with cloth or paper towels until dry; or use a salad spinner. The soaking will do the trick every time for slightly wilted or "soft" leaves. If I have time, I like to soak even healthy looking leaves, since it always makes them more crisp.

After patting dry, the lettuce can be stored wrapped in a moist towel or several layers of paper towels (use the towels you used to dry the leaves, as they will be moist already) and the whole thing enclosed in a plastic bag. The lettuce will remain crisp in the refrigerator for one to two weeks. This is a very convenient way to store lettuce, since the lettuce is ready when you are and you do not have to go through the whole process of washing and drying lettuce each time you want a salad.

Tear the lettuce leaves with your hands; do not use a knife. I prefer pieces that fit into the mouth, although I have often been served whole leaves of lettuce and nothing but a fork to eat them with.

Add only enough dressing to coat each piece; the salad should not be swimming in dressing. Add the dressing immediately before you serve the salad, since the vinegar could wilt the lettuce if allowed to sit too long. Also, it is tastier to add dressing to the whole batch and toss, rather than on individual servings.

Sometimes you will want to serve a salad with just greens (different varieties of lettuce) in it. Other times you will want to add other vegetables. Some suggestions for vegetables to add to salads are listed in the ingredient columns on the opposite page.

Feel free to add anything you want, but remember that the vegetables should all be cut to a reasonable size. This means that they should be small enough to blend with the other ingredients in one bite. Many times, the individual vegetable pieces are so large that you can only eat one vegetable at a time. It's nice if the pieces are small enough that you can get a little carrot, avocado, red pepper, and lettuce in a single bite. But then again, some like them big.

# Basic Vinaigrette

*It is so simple to make a tasty salad dressing at home that I frequently wonder why people buy it bottled. Basic vinaigrette (oil and vinegar) is a useful dressing to be able to make, and experimenting with a variety of oils and vinegar will yield a different product each time. It can also be flavored with garlic, herbs, mustard, and grated onion.*

*NOTE: Vinegars have various degrees of acidity, so the amount of oil added will differ depending on what you use. Rice and balsamic vinegar are milder, and can be mixed with less oil than wine vinegars. Personal preference for tangy or not-so-tangy dressings will also determine the amount of oil to use.*

*1 part vinegar of choice
    (red or white wine, balsamic,
    rice, or herbal)*
*2 - 3 parts oil of choice
    (extra virgin olive, walnut,
    safflower, canola, etc. Please,
    no peanut oil.)*

Place the vinegar in a bowl with the salt and pepper. Whipping with a wire whisk, add the oil in a thin, slow, steady stream until it emulsifies and thickens. (This is hard to do without a whisk. Using one will keep the dressing from separating quickly.) Adjust seasoning as necessary. It can be used immediately or stored for later use (whisk again before serving.

*Garlic Vinaigrette*: Mash 1 clove of garlic for each 1/2 cup of vinaigrette and add to the dressing. Allow to sit for at least 1 hour before serving. Remove garlic before pouring on salad. Another idea is to finely mince the garlic (or use a garlic press) and add to the vinegar before adding the oil. It can then be served immediately.

*Herb Vinaigrette*: Fresh herbs are preferable to dried, but dried will do. Finely mince herbs of choice (tarragon, dill, basil, marjoram, thyme, etc.). Use (a total of) 2 - 3 Tbsp. for each 1/2 cup of dressing. Add to the vinegar before whisking in the salt. For dried herbs, use (a total of) 2 teaspoons for each 1/2 cup.

*Mustard Vinaigrette*: Add 3 Tbsp. Dijon mustard to the vinegar for each 1/2 cup of dressing before whisking in the oil.

*Onion Vinaigrettte*: Add 1 Tbsp. grated onion to the vinegar for each 1/2 cup of dressing before adding the oil.

# Orange-Soy Dressing

*A wonderful, unusual combination perfect for tender leaves of Boston or butterhead lettuce tossed together with ripe avocado and, perhaps, a few roasted pecans. It is also excellent with Belgian endive, avocado, orange pieces, and pecans.*

It's very important to squeeze the orange juice right before using or it will lack the necessary aroma and flavor. Mix the juice, soy sauce, and vinegar together, then whisk in the safflower oil slowly until thickened.

*Per 1 Tbsp. serving: Calories: 67, Protein: 0 gm., Fat: 7 gm., Carbohydrates: 1 gm.*

*California Salad:* Although excellent over tender greens, this dressing can also be used over a mixture of shredded cabbage and carrots, diced avocados, orange pieces, and lightly toasted sunflower seeds. This is a nice, light alternative to cole slaw.

*Makes 1/2 cup*

*1/4 cup freshly squeezed orange juice*

*1 1/2 Tbsp. soy sauce*

*1 Tbsp. rice vinegar (available at natural food or Japanese grocers)*

*1/4 cup safflower or other light oil*

# Spicy Oriental Dressing

Makes 3/4 cup

1/4 cup soy sauce

1/2 tsp. cayenne pepper

3 Tbsp. mirin

3 Tbsp. rice vinegar

1/4 cup salad oil

*For those who like it slightly hot, this is a good dressing for a mixed green salad. Adjust the amount of cayenne pepper to suit your taste.*

Mix the soy sauce, cayenne pepper, mirin, and rice vinegar. While whisking, add the salad oil a little at a time until it all emulsifies.

*Per 1 Tbsp. serving: Calories: 56, Protein: 0 gm., Fat: 5 gm., Carbohydrates: 4 gm.*

# Tofu Sour Cream

Blend all ingredients together until thick and smooth.

*Per 1 Tbsp. serving: Calories: 38, Protein: 1 gm., Fat: 4 gm., Carbohydrates: 1 gm.*

*Makes 1 1/4 cups*

*14 - 16 oz. silken tofu
   (no other will do for this)*
*4 Tbsp. light salad oil
   (safflower, canola, etc.)*
*2 Tbsp. lemon juice*
*salt to taste*

# Tofu Mayonnaise

Makes 1 1/4 cups

1 lb. tofu, preferably silken
    (for a smoother texture)
3 - 4  Tbsp. salad or olive oil
2 - 3 Tbsp. white wine vinegar
    (other vinegar may be substi-
    tuted)
salt to taste
1/2 tsp. powdered
    or 2 tsp. prepared mustard
    (optional)

*A basic dressing and ingredient to other recipes.*

Blend all the ingredients in a food processor until smooth and thick. This will keep for two weeks under refrigeration and can be used for sandwiches, salads, and as a base for other dressings.

*Per 1 Tbsp. serving: Calories: 39, Protein: 2 gm., Fat: 3 gm., Carbohydrates: 1 gm.*

# Creamy Caper and Parsley Dressing

*Very pretty over steamed, chilled slices of Japanese kabocha or butternut squash.*

Blend until thick and smooth. Chill until serving time.

*Per serving: Calories: 23, Protein: 1 gm., Fat: 2 gm., Carbohydrates: 1 gm.*

*Makes about 1 cup*

*1/2 cup tofu mayonnaise*
*2 Tbsp. (or more) capers*
*1/2 cup chopped parsley*
*1/4 cup soy milk*
*salt to taste*

# Tofu Thousand Island Dressing

*Makes 1 1/2 cups*

*1/3 lb. tofu*

*4 Tbsp. tomato paste*

*2 - 3 Tbsp. olive oil*

*3 Tbsp. red wine vinegar*

*1 Tbsp. honey*

*1 Tbsp. soy sauce*

*1 clove garlic (optional)*

*salt and pepper to taste (optional)*

*Much lower in calories than the commercial dressings, so feel free to use it liberally.*

Blend all ingredients until smooth and creamy. (Finely chopped green pepper and onion may be added.)

*Per 1 Tbsp. serving: Calories: 26, Protein: 1 gm., Fat: 2 gm., Carbohydrates: 2 gm.*

# Mediterranean Pasta Salad

*Serves 4-6*

Prepare the tofu "feta" cheese by cutting or tearing the tofu into 1/2" chunks. Add the salt and enough olive oil to cover the chunks. Cover and marinate 12 to 24 hours. Drain to use. Some oil will cling to pieces.

For the salad, reconstitute the dried tomatoes with water and drain. Toss all the salad ingredients lightly. Mix the dressing ingredients and combine with the tofu "feta" cheese. Add the dressing to the salad.

*Per serving: Calories: 376, Protein: 14 gm., Fat: 6 gm.,Carbohydrates: 54 gm.*

*Tofu "Feta" Cheese:*
1 cup Tofu Cheese, page 32
olive oil to cover
1 - 2 tsp. salt

*The Salad:*
4 cups cooked vegetable spirals,
    or other noodles
1/2 cup Greek Kalamata olives
1/3 cup sun-dried tomatoes
1/3 cup fresh basil leaves, thinly
    slivered
1 cup cherry tomatoes, halves
1 small pepper, red, green, or
    yellow, thinly sliced into rings
1/2 cup red onion, thinly sliced

*The Dressing:*
2 cloves garlic, finely minced
1/4 cup Kalamata olive brine
2 - 3 Tbsp. balsamic vinegar
salt and pepper to taste

# On Steaming Vegetables

In my home we often eat nothing but a plate filled with an array of steamed vegetables in season, and we delight in their sweetness and succulence each time. If the vegetables are really at the peak of their season, and especially if they are organic, they will be absolutely delicious completely unadorned. However, they can be enhanced by a light seasoning. Butter has been a favorite for Americans, while Japanese prefer soy sauce; I suggest a little olive oil and lemon, or olive oil and soy sauce, keeping a light touch and not dousing the vegetables. Freshly picked herbs can be chopped and sprinkled on, as can salt and pepper. When the taste buds crave some more excitement, you can make two or three dipping sauces and dip away as you eat your vegetables with some brown rice. Teriyaki sauce, tahini sauce, and a curry sauce would be possibilities.

Steam a variety of vegetables, using a combination of leafy, stalk, and root varieties, and strive for a color combination that will provide both eye appeal and nutritional value. Spinach, kale, collard greens, mustard greens, and chard are all wonderful steamed, and you will find that spinach does not become one mushy lump if steamed and not boiled. Broccoli, cauliflower, cabbage, and members of the squash family, including pumpkin, can all be sliced and steamed. Even potatoes are excellent steamed, as are onions cut into thick rings. Celery is the one choice I have not found to be as good as the others. Whatever vegetables you use, steam them only until they are tender-crisp, then remove from the steamer immediately to prevent further cooking. Steaming times will vary depending on the type of vegetable and how you have cut them, so cook the harder vegetables first, and add leafy and other quick-cooking vegetables later so that they all finish at relatively the same time.

I prefer a bamboo steamer that can be stacked or layered to clumsy metal steamers. The bamboo steamers can be purchased in most cook ware shops or import stores and are relatively inexpensive—Chinese groceries carry them sometimes, too. Place them in a large pot or skillet with an inch of water in it and turn the heat to high. When the water boils, turn the heat down and cook the vegetables until tender.

# Greco-Japanese Style Spinach

*Serves 4*

1/3 cup pine nuts (or more,
    according to taste), roughly
    chopped

2 Tbsp. olive oil

2 Tbsp. soy sauce

1 Tbsp. mirin

1 - 2 Tbsp. lemon juice

1 bunch spinach, lightly steamed

*Well, I figured, with all the strange combinations in food these days, why not Greek and Japanese? Actually, it works and it's simple!*

Sauté the pine nuts in the olive oil until lightly browned. Add the soy sauce, mirin, and lemon juice, then pour over the lightly steamed, hot spinach.

*Per serving: Calories: 161, Protein: 5 gm., Fat: 13 gm., Carbohydrates: 9 gm.*

# Vegetables in Ginger Cream Sauce

Serves 6

*A creamy and slightly sweet sauce with the pep of ginger smothers chunks of tender veggies. Use your own combination of vegetables but it's nice to have something that's white, and something that is red or orange in it.*

Combine the water, wine, and onion in a saucepan with a tight fitting lid and cook until the onion is relatively tender. Add the chunks of vegetables and continue cooking, covered, until they are tender-crisp (do not overcook). Remove the vegetables with a slotted spoon or drain through a colander, reserving the liquid. Measure the liquid. If it has not been reduced to 3/4 of a cup, return it to the pot and boil down rapidly.

Melt 1 1/2 Tbsp. margarine in a small saucepan and add the flour to it to make a roux, stirring constantly over the low heat (if you are using the same pot you cooked the vegetables in, it's a good idea to rinse it out and wipe it dry before going onto this step so that the margarine does not burn). Cook for a minute or two. Add the hot reduced stock from the vegetables, whisking all the while, and then the soy milk and ginger. Continue stirring and cooking until thick and creamy. Season with salt and pepper and toss with the hot vegetables. Serve!

This is also good reheated the next day.

*Per serving: Calories: 98, Protein: 4 gm., Fat: 4 gm., Carbohydrates: 12 gm.*

1 1/2 cups water

1/2 cup white wine

1 onion, cut into eighths

1/2 to 2/3 cup each cauliflower,
    parsnips, yams, rutabagas,
    carrots or mushrooms,
    all cut into large chunks

1 1/2 Tbsp. margarine or oil

2 Tbsp. flour

1 cup rich soy milk

1 - 3 tsp. freshly grated ginger

salt and white pepper to taste

# Curried Sweet Potato Cakes

*Serves 4 - 6*

2 large sweet potatoes or yams,
  steamed, baked or microwaved
  until soft
3 tsp. freshly grated ginger
2 - 3 tsp. curry powder
2 tsp. soy sauce
2 tsp. ground coriander
approx. 1/2 cup soy milk

*Try these slightly spicy and rich-tasting patties in place of the traditional candied yams for Thanksgiving or Christmas (or anytime, for that matter).*

Peel the cooked sweet potato, cut up into chunks and process with the other ingredients in a food processor until smooth. The mixture should be firm enough to handle and shape. Form into patties and sauté on both sides in margarine until crispy on both sides.

*Per serving: Calories: 105, Protein: 2 gm., Fat: 0 gm., Carbohydrates: 23 gm.*

# Minted Carrots

This is my favorite way to serve carrots; easy to prepare, with a very interesting and refreshing flavor. I like to serve them for Thanksgiving and Christmas.

Cut the carrots into slices or sticks as desired, and steam until tender. Toss with the remaining ingredients while the carrots are still hot and serve immediately.

*Per Serving: Calories: 73, Protein: 1 gm., Fat: 4 gm., Carbohydrates: 8 gm.*

*Serves 4-6*

1 lb. carrots

2 Tbsp. fresh mint, chopped

2 Tbsp. margarine

2 Tbsp. orange juice

1 tsp. (or slightly more) honey

salt and pepper to taste

# Eggplant and Mushrooms in Red Wine

*Serves 4*

1 medium eggplant

2 Tbsp. olive oil

1/4 lb. small button mushrooms

1/2 cup red wine

2 - 3 Tbsp. soy sauce

2 Tbsp. mirin

*A dark and delicious concoction.*

Cut the eggplant into 1/2" cubes and sprinkle generously with salt. Let it drain in a colander for twenty to thirty minutes, then rinse and pat dry with paper towels. Heat the olive oil in a pan and sauté the eggplants until slightly tender, then add the mushrooms and continue sautéing for 3 to 4 minutes. Add the red wine, soy sauce, and mirin, cover with a tight fitting lid, and stew slowly until only a few tablespoons of liquid remain in the pan and the vegetables are nearly black in appearance.

*Per serving: Calories: 149, Protein: 3 gm., Fat: 7 gm., Carbohydrates:17 gm.*

# Steamed Eggplant with Tomatoes and Ginger

*Here is a completely fat-free and simple-to-make vegetable side dish with an unusual flavor. This can also be eaten cold the next day.*

Stew the tomatoes, onion and garlic in a saucepan with a tight fitting lid until the onion is soft. Steam the eggplant lightly until a fork pierces easily but do not allow it to get mushy or lose shape. Add the eggplant, ginger, and the basil to the saucepan with the tomato mixture and cook another 5 to 6 minutes to allow flavors to mingle.

*Per serving: Calories: 109, Protein: 5 gm., Fat: 0 gm., Carbohydrates: 24 gm.*

*Serves 4*

2 large tomatoes, chopped

1 medium onion, chopped

2 cloves garlic, minced

1 medium eggplant, cut into
   large chunks (not peeled)

1 Tbsp. freshly grated ginger

1/4 tsp. basil

# Gâteau d'Aubergines Gratin

*Serves 4*

1 large eggplant

2 - 3 Tbsp. olive oil for sautéing

salt and dried basil

1 1/2 cups dry, fine wholewheat
   breadcrumbs

2 - 3 Tbsp. tablespoons olive oil

2 cloves garlic, finely minced

1/2 tsp. each basil, marjoram,
   and oregano or rosemary

salt and pepper to taste

*This is surely a rich and delicious way to serve eggplant.*

Slice the eggplant into 1/3" slices and sprinkle with salt. Place in a colander and allow to drain for twenty to thirty minutes. Scrape the juices and salt off the surfaces of the eggplant slices with a knife and place on an oiled baking sheet. Sprinkle the tops with salt and a little basil. Grill under a broiler until brown, then turn over and grill the other side but do not allow the slices to burn or become crispy.

In an 8" baking dish, put down a layer of grilled eggplant. Mix the breadcrumbs with the garlic, herbs, olive oil to dampen, and salt and pepper, and sprinkle 1/4 of this on top of the first layer of eggplants. Keep repeating this process of alternating eggplant slices with the bread crumb mixture until all is gone. The top layer should be the breadcrumbs, so you should have about 4 layers of eggplant and 4 of the breadcrumbs. Press down on top to compact it slightly and bake in a preheated 350° oven for 15 to 20 minutes. Cut into pieces as if you were cutting a cake.

*Per serving: Calories: 372, Protein: 9 gm., Fat: 18 gm., Carbohydrates: 44 gm.*

# Garlic Rice

*Transform leftover brown rice into a pretty and flavorful dish that can accompany all types of entrees from loaves and casseroles, and to Mexican dishes.*

Combine all the ingredients in a pyrex or ceramic baking dish, cover with aluminum foil, and bake in a 350° oven for 30 minutes, or until heated through. This may also be microwaved.

*Per serving: Calories: 189, Protein: 3 gm., Fat: 10 gm., Carbohydrates: 21 gm.*

*Serves 6*

3 cups cooked brown rice,
   either cold or hot

3/4 cup to 1 cup parsley,
   finely minced

5 - 6 cloves garlic, finely minced

1/2 tsp. salt

1/3 cup melted margarine
   or low-calorie butter substitute

# Orange-Maple Yams

Serves 4-6

See photo on page 150.

3 lbs. yams

6 Tbsp. maple syrup

4 Tbsp. frozen concentrated
  orange juice

2 - 4 Tbsp. margarine or butter
  (optional)

*Not overly sweet, this harmonious combination of flavors complements a holiday "bird" nicely (see Great Gluten Turkey, pages 158-9). It can also be served at any other time of the year.*

Scrub the yams well and bake in a 350° oven until a fork pierces through easily (anywhere from 30 - 60 minutes depending on size). If desired, the yams can be baked hours or even the day before serving. Allow to cool enough to handle, then peel. Mash the yams in a bowl, combine with the maple syrup and orange juice and mix well. Place in a buttered casserole or baking dish, and if desired, dot with butter or margarine. Cover with aluminum foil and bake at 350° until heated through.

*Per serving: Calories: 455, Protein: 9 gm., Fat: 0 gm., Carbohydrates: 106 gm.*

# Dilly Cabbage with Carrots

*A warm version of sauerkraut that isn't so sour.*

Heat the oil in a saucepan and add the cabbage and carrots. Cover and cook over a low flame, stirring occasionally, for about five minutes or until slightly tender. Add the apple juice, vinegar, and dill weed, cover again, and cook until tender. Add the soy sauce, cook another two minutes, and serve.

*Per servings: Calories: 59, Protein: 2 gm., Fat: 1 gm., Carbohydrates: 12 gm.*

*Serves 4 - 6*

1/2 head cabbage, sliced thin or shredded

2 carrots, sliced into very thin sticks

1 tsp. oil

1/2 cup apple juice

2 Tbsp. red wine vinegar

2 tsp. dill weed (dried)

1 - 2 Tbsp. soy sauce

# Go Ahead and Indulge:

## Serious Desserts That Play Lightly on Your Heart

Even the most committed dieter or natural food aficionado occasionally breaks down in front of a rich, decadent dessert. Unfortunately, "natural" substitutes (the colorless, dry concoctions that try to pass for sweet treats in health food stores) do not always satisfy that particular craving we mortals sometimes have for indulgence. The bottom line is that people eat desserts because they taste good, not for any nutritional benefit. This is not to say that they can't be nutritious or healthy, but simply that they shouldn't have to taste too "healthy." Thus, here is a collection of desserts ranging from fruit dishes to richer mousses and tarts that make no apologies for the way they taste. They are, however, all healthy, and I do extend my apologies to anyone out there who might be disturbed by that and claim that I was destroying their ability to enjoy these treats.

A note about sweeteners: All of the following recipes can be sweetened with honey. Barley malt, rice syrup, or concentrated fruit juice can be used in place of honey in many of the recipes, and are indicated where applicable. If you object to the use of honey, feel free to experiment with other natural sweeteners even where they are not indicated. Again, personal taste will often dictate how sweet a dessert should be, so feel free to increase the amount of sweetener used.

# Chestnut Tart

*Serves 6*

1/2 cup cashew milk (see page 15)

1 cup cooked chestnut meats

8 oz. tofu

1/3 cup honey, barley malt, rice
    syrup, or concentrated fruit
    juice

1 tsp. vanilla

2 Tbsp. brandy or cognac

1/2 tsp. grated orange peel

1 Tbsp. arrowroot or kuzu

10 - 15 additional whole chest-
    nuts*

1 unbaked 8" pie crust of your
    choice

*These must not be broken into
    pieces—if you are cooking
    your own, peel very carefully.
    Otherwise, use canned or
    bottled.*

*Chestnuts are widely appreciated as an ingredient in desserts in Europe and Japan, although they are not often used in America. Actually, their subtle sweetness lends itself to a variety of dishes, and they are extremely high in complex carbohydrates and protein to boot. Dried chestnuts are inadequate for this; use fresh, or if this is too much trouble, canned or bottled ones—these should be in water, not heavy syrup.*

*This tart is quite pleasant with a cup of hot tea.*

Heat the cashew milk and one cup of chestnuts together in a small saucepan. Purée in a food processor until smooth. Add the tofu, honey, vanilla, brandy, orange peel, and arrowroot and purée again until smooth. Pour into the unbaked pie shell and arrange the 10 to 15 whole chestnuts on it decoratively. Bake in a 425° oven for 15 minutes, then lower the temperature to 350° and continue baking for an additional 25 - 30 minutes.

Serve warm, at room temperature, or chilled. You may drizzle on some honey, or brush the top with a syrup made by heating frozen concentrated orange juice with honey, if you like.

A note on cooking chestnuts: If you are going to prepare the nutmeats from fresh chestnuts, refer to the instructions in the Baked Apple Filled with Chestnut Purée recipe on pages 218-9. The chestnuts that are to be pureed can be scooped out with a spoon as described. The ones for decorating, however, must be whole. Also, these may be cooked for a few minutes in a simple honey-water mixture to sweeten further, if desired. Although freshly cooked chestnuts are wonderful, perfectly adequate canned or bottled ones are available and greatly expedite the recipe.

*Per serving: Calories: 366, Protein: 8 gm., Fat: 13 gm., Carbohydrates: 54 gm.*

*Christmas Pudding, pg. 224*

# Cheesy Walnut Raisin Crêpes

*These are nice for a Sunday brunch or a simple dessert. The tofu comes out tasting like ricotta or cottage cheese, and it can be served as is, or with maple syrup, honey, or Citrus Brandy Sauce, pg. 244. If you have frozen crêpes on hand (which you can make ahead of time and freeze), the dish is a breeze to assemble.*

Mash the tofu with a fork until it resembles ricotta cheese. Add the sweetener, raisins, nuts, and spices, and mix well. Fill the crêpes as desired (either roll up or fold into quarters) and sauté lightly in margarine over low heat until lightly browned and heated through. Alternately, the crêpes can be heated in a microwave or conventional oven. If you use a conventional oven, cover them with aluminum foil to prevent drying and hardening.

Top with sauce or syrup of choice and serve immediately.

*Per serving: Calories: 254, Protein: 10 gm., Fat: 11 gm., Carbohydrates: 32 gm.*

*Serves 4-6*

12 oz. firm tofu

3 Tbsp. honey or maple syrup

1/3 cup currants
   or raisins

1/3 cup walnuts, lightly toasted
   and chopped

1/4 cup almonds, lightly toasted
   and slivered (optional)

1/4 tsp. nutmeg, freshly grated

a dash or two of cinnamon

Have ready:
4 - 6 large crêpes

*Chocolate Almond Raspberry Torte, pgs. 204-5*

# Chocolate (Carob) Almond Raspberry Torte

Serves 12

See photo on page 202.

**For the Layers:**

1/2 cup margarine
   (preferably unsalted),
     or 1/2 cup oil minus 2 Tbsp.

2/3 cup honey or barley malt

3 Tbsp. brandy

7 oz. blanched almond meal
   (finely ground almonds)

2 cups semi-dried okara
   (see page 17)

2/3 cup soy milk

6 Tbsp. cocoa or carob powder

2 1/2 tsp. aluminum-free baking
   powder

**Raspberry Filling**

8 oz. raspberries

1/3 cup honey
 or 1/2 cup frozen concentrated
   apple juice

2 Tbsp. cornstarch

2 - 3 Tbsp. water

*This rich, decadent, special-occasion treat contains no eggs, dairy products, or flour, and is equally delicious made with either chocolate or carob (for carob, less sweetener may be used since carob is naturally sweet). Okara, the high-fiber part of the soybean that is a by-product of tofu processing, helps to produce a moist, delicate cake. It can either be made at home (just make some tofu and you will end up with quite a bit), purchased from a local tofu manufacturer, or ordered from the address on page 17.*

Pre-heat the oven to 350°.

To prepare the layers, cream the margarine with the honey, and then add the brandy, mixing well. Stir in the almond meal and okara, mixing well, then add the soy milk. Sift the cocoa or carob powder with the baking powder, and mix in well. (This batter will resemble a very soft, moist cookie dough). Line a cookie sheet with baking paper, divide the batter into two portions, patting out two 7" - 7 1/2" circles on the sheet (two 8" springform pans lined with baking paper may also be used—do not attempt to use regular cake pans or the layers will crumble upon removal!). Bake for 25 minutes until the edges are beginning to darken. They will expand by an inch or more in diameter. Allow to cool completely before handling.

While the layers are baking, prepare the Raspberry Filling. Set aside a few raspberries for garnish, and combine the rest with the honey or apple juice in a saucepan. Bring to a boil, reduce heat, and simmer for about ten minutes, stirring occasionally, until the raspberries have dissolved. Mix the water and cornstarch over low heat, add to the raspberries to thicken. Set aside to cool.

To prepare the Chocolate Ganache melt the chocolate or carob chips over (not in) hot water. Combine all the ingredients in a food processor and blend until absolutely creamy. Taste for sweetness, adding more honey or barley malt if desired. Use this soon after making or it will stiffen too much to spread.

To assemble the cake, place one layer upside-down on a platter with the baking paper still intact. Peel off the paper and spread about 1/3 of the ganache evenly over the layer, then place the other cake layer on top and peel off the paper gently. Spread the raspberry "jam" on top. Trim the sides with a very sharp knife and cover completely with most of the remaining ganache, saving about 1/3 - 1/2 cup for decorating the top.

To decorate, pipe rosettes on top with a pastry bag or tube. Garnish, if desired, with chocolate rolls or shavings, and dust lightly with cornstarch.

*Optional Chocolate Rolls or Shavings:* Melt the chocolate or carob and pour onto a marble slab or similar cold, hard surface. Chill completely, then scrape with a vegetable peeler to form rolls or shavings.

*Per serving: Calories: 498, Protein: 13 gm., Fat: 23 gm., Carbohydrates: 55*

*Chocolate Ganache:*
*20 oz. tofu*
*(if firm, add 1/2 cup soy milk)*
*1/2 cup honey*
*or 3/4 cup barley malt*
*6 oz. unsweetened chocolate*
*(or carob chips)*
*1/3 cup cocoa or carob powder*
*1 tsp. vanilla*
*2 Tbsp. brandy*

*Chocolate Rolls or Shavings*
*(for garnish—optional):*
*2 oz. bittersweet chocolate or carob chips (if using chocolate, try a dairy-free, white sugar - free variety, if available)*

# Fresh Strawberry Almond Tart

Serves 8

See photo on page 220.

1 cup blanched almonds
   or almond meal
1/2 - 3/4 cup water
   (whole, blanched almonds need
   more than almond meal)
3 - 5 Tbsp. honey
2 Tbsp. safflower oil (optional)
2 Tbsp. kirschwasser,
   or 2 Tbsp. water and several
   drops lemon juice
2 Tbsp. kuzu, 3 Tbsp. arrowroot,
   or 2 - 3 Tbsp. cornstarch
   (dissolved in water)
4 1/2 cups fresh, ripe, sweet
   strawberries in season
1 tsp. vanilla
3 - 4 more Tbsp. honey
1 Tbsp. more arrowroot or kuzu

Have ready:
1 recipe Almond Pastry,
   prebaked (page 234),
   or whole wheat pie crust

*What can I say about this? If I were to choose one dessert for my Last Meal, this would be it. It is, simply put, just absolutely wonderful. Strawberries must be fresh, ripe, and sweet. Don't attempt this tart with frozen or unripe, unsweetened strawberries or you'll be gravely disappointed.*

First, make an almond pastry cream. Combine the almonds and water in a blender or food processor (a blender will probably produce a smoother cream) and blend until smooth and creamy, adding more water if necessary. Add the honey, oil, vanilla and 1 tablespoon of the kirshwasser and continue blending; it should be absolutely smooth. Pour it into a small saucepan and place over low heat, stirring constantly. Dissolve the 2 Tbsp. of arrowroot in a small amount of water, and when the almond cream comes to a boil, add it, stirring constantly until the mixture thickens. Remove from heat and allow to cool. Pour a thin layer of soy milk on top to prevent a skin from forming.

Wash and hull all the strawberries. In order to make the tart as visually appealing as possible, it is best if the strawberries are generally the same size; try to separate 3 cups of berries that are roughly equal in size. The remaining 1 1/2 cups will be pureed to make a glaze, and hence can be assorted sizes and shapes, as well as slightly overripe. For the glaze, combine the 1 1/2 cups of (slightly inferior) strawberries and the 3 - 4 tablespoons of honey in a saucepan and cook, covered, for ten to fifteen minutes, or until juices have been exuded and it is a bright, beautiful red. Pour this into a blender and purée until smooth. Pour this back into the saucepan, reheat, and thicken with 1 Tbsp. of arrowroot dissolved in the remaining kirschwasser or water with a few drops of lemon juice. It should be a light, clear, bright red sauce.

To assemble the tart, spread the almond pastry cream in the prebaked crust. Arrange the whole strawberries (if they are large, you may want to cut them in half) attractively over the pastry cream. With a spoon or pastry brush, cover up the tart with the strawberry glaze while it is still hot (the glaze will set as it cools). Chill for 3 - 4 hours before serving. If you want to make this dessert the day before serving, it is best to use a short crust as it will stay crisp. The delicate whole-wheat pie crust tends to soften if left too long in the refrigerator (24 hours).

*Per serving: Calories: 443, Protein: 9 gm., Fat: 28 gm., Carbohydrates: 44 gm.*

# Jellied Peach Jewels

Serves 4

1 pint apple juice

3/4 bar or 3/4 tsp. powdered agar

1 large peach, peeled and chopped
   into 1/2-inch chunks

juice of 1/2 lemon

2 Tbsp. honey

*Extremely light, refreshing, and easy to make. Peeling a peach is simple if you plunge it in boiling water for 20 seconds—the skin slips right off.*

Dissolve the agar in the apple juice as described on page 10. Add the peach to the apple juice and continue to boil for another 30 seconds. Add the lemon juice and honey and cook another moment (long enough to dissolve the honey), and then pour into individual parfait or wine glasses. Chill until set.

If desired, make a half-recipe of the Cashew Cheesecake, page 217, pour it in the bottom of individual dishes, and then pour the jellied peaches on top for a two-layer summer treat.

*Per serving: Calories: 103, Protein: 0 gm., Fat: 0 gm., Carbohydrates: 26 gm.*

# Glistening Poached Pears

*Delightfully easy to make and a joy to eat, these jewel-like glistening pears will make a fine, light dessert after a rich meal.*

Wash the pears and place in a large pot. Add the juice, wine, honey, and lemon. Cover and simmer until the pears are tender, about 30 minutes.

Dissolve the arrowroot, kuzu, or cornstarch in a small amount of water and add to the liquid in the pot over low heat, stirring constantly, until it thickens to a light glaze.

Serve hot, or allow to cool slightly to just warm, and decorate with a sprig of mint, if desired.

*Per serving: Calories: 297, Protein: 1 gm., Fat: 0 gm., Carbohydrates: 71 gm.*

*Serves 6*

*6 Bosc pears, medium firm*
  *(do not use mushy ones)*
*1 qt. cherry juice*
*1 cup red wine*
*1/3 cup honey*
*1/2 lemon, sliced*
*2 Tbsp. kuzu,*
  *or 3 Tbsp. cornstarch*
  *or arrowroot, dissolved in a*
  *small amount of water*

# Fresh Figs Stewed in Red Wine

*Serves 4*

*8 large fresh figs*

*1 1/2 cups red wine*

*1/4 cup currants*

*3 Tbsp. honey*

   *or 1/4 cup concentrated apple*

   *or grape juice*

*juice and rind of one lemon*

*1 cinnamon stick*

   *or 5 whole cloves (optional)*

*Fresh figs are rarely seen in the United States, a shame since they are among the most luscious of fruit. Although rather unattractive on the outside, a really ripe, fresh fig will reveal beautifully succulent purple flesh once split open with your fingers. This dessert is simple and can be a delicious ending for a summer meal.*

To prepare the lemon rind simply peel the thin, yellow surface—there's no need to grate it. Combine all the ingredients in a saucepan with a tight fitting lid and simmer gently for twenty minutes. Serve warm or chilled. If desired, a little Tofu Cashew Crème, page 220, may be served alongside.

*Per serving: Calories: 229, Protein: 1 gm., Fat: 0 gm., Carbohydrates: 48 gm.*

# Orange Bavarian

*Creamy, sweet, delightful.*

Grate the orange zest, and juice both the orange and lemon. Combine the zest, the two juices, and 1/4 cup honey in a small saucepan and place it over medium heat. Dissolve the cornstarch or kuzu in a small amount of water. When the juice mixture comes to a boil, add the cornstarch mixture in a steady stream while stirring constantly. Lower the heat and continue cooking until clear and very thick, stirring all the while. Remove from heat.

Place the tofu, oil, orange liqueur, and the remaining honey in a food processor and blend until smooth and creamy. Add the orange custard to this and blend for only a few moments at low speed to combine gently (do not overblend).

Dissolve the agar in the orange juice, using the method described on page 10, and add to the mixture in the food processor. Once again, blend for another few moments, only long enough to combine gently. DO NOT OVERBLEND OR THE TEXTURE WILL BE DESTROYED. Pour into wine or parfait glasses and chill 3 - 4 hours or overnight until set. If desired, top with Tofu or Cashew Crème, page 220.

*Per serving: Calories: 212, Protein: 6 gm., Fat: 3 gm., Carbohydrates: 44 gm.*

Serves 4

1 large orange

1 lemon

1/4 cup honey, plus 2 - 3 Tbsp.

3 Tbsp. cornstarch or kuzu, plus small amount of water to dissolve it

12 oz. silken tofu

3 Tbsp. safflower or canola oil (optional)

2 Tbsp. Grand Marnier or other orange liqueur

1/2 cup orange juice

1/2 bar or 1/2 tsp. powdered agar

# Tropical Coconut Banana Ice Cream or Sauce

*Serves 4*

12 oz. tofu

3 ripe bananas
    (should be spotty brown)

1 cup unsweetened coconut,
    grated or flaked

1/2 cup soy milk

2 tsp. vanilla

1 Tbsp. dark rum (optional)

4 Tbsp. salad oil (optional)

honey to taste
    (a few tablespoons—depends
    on sweetness of bananas and
    coconut)

Blend all ingredients together in a food processor until smooth. If you have an ice cream maker, follow the manufacturer's instructions for freezing. Otherwise, place the mixture in a bowl in a freezer until semi-hard. Then homogenize it by creaming it in a food processor and freeze again until firm.

*Coconut Banana Sauce* (for banana bread, pound cake, leftover cake or brownie chunks): Use only half the amount of tofu, coconut, and banana. Delete the salad oil. Sweeten to taste with honey as for ice cream Purée all in a blender or food processor, and serve immediately.

*Per serving: Calories: 276, Protein: 10 gm., Fat: 17 gm., Carbohydrates: 26 gm.*

# A Different Pumpkin Ice Cream

*A wonderful tofu-based ice cream with an unusual, complex character. The undertones of orange and spice make this special—serve it in champagne glasses with a sprig of mint on top.*

Serves 4

Combine all the ingredients except the orange juice and agar in a food processor or blender and blend until very smooth and creamy. Dissolve the agar in the orange juice as described on page 10 and add it to the ingredients in the blender, blending once again. If you have an ice cream maker, follow the manufacturer's instructions for churning. Otherwise, pour into a bowl and place in the freezer until completely frozen. Remove from the freezer, allow to soften slightly, then chop into large chunks and process in the food processor until perfectly creamy and homogenized. It can then be served immediately or refrozen.

*Per serving: Calories: 326, Protein: 9 gm., Fat: 18 gm., Carbohydrates: 31 gm.*

14 oz. tofu

1 cup cooked butternut squash,
    canned pumpkin, or Japanese
    pumpkin (kabocha), preferably
    the latter

4 Tbsp. bland oil
    (canola or safflower is fine)

4 Tbsp. or more honey,
    depending on the sweetness of
    squash used

2 Tbsp. Grand Marnier or other
    orange liqueur

zest of 3/4 of one orange rind

1/2 tsp. lemon zest

scant 1/2 tsp. cinnamon

scant 1/4 tsp. nutmeg

1/2 cup orange juice,
    freshly squeezed

1/2 bar or 1/2 tsp. powdered agar

# Strawberry Mousse Parfait

Serves 6

2 pints fresh strawberries,
  washed and hulled

1/2 cup blanched almonds or
  almond meal (almond meal
  purées faster)

1/2 cup water

2 Tbsp. oil (optional - for richer
  flavor)

2 Tbsp. kirshwasser
  or 1/2 Tbsp. lemon juice
  and 1 Tbsp. rum)

12 oz. tofu, pressed (see page 24)

1/3 cup honey (or more,
  depending on sweetness of
  strawberries)

2 Tbsp. arrowroot, cornstarch, or
  kuzu plus 1 - 2 Tbsp. of water
  to dissolve it

1/2 bar or 1/2 tsp. powdered agar

1 recipe Tofu Crème of choice,
  page 218

*Delicate, sweet, rich, and pretty.*

Reserve 6 - 8 nicely shaped strawberries for decorating the top (the hulls can be left on these, if desired).

In a blender make an almond cream by puréeing the almonds, water, oil, and kirshwasser until absolutely smooth (a blender works better than a food processor for this). Pour this into a large bowl.

In the same blender, purée 1 pint of the strawberries with the honey and tofu until smooth. Add to the almond cream and combine well with a whisk.

Rinse out the blender. Purée the other pint of strawberries with a small amount of water. You should have about 1 cup of juice. Pour this into a saucepan and dissolve the agar in it as described on page 10. After it has been dissolved turn the heat down low and add the arrowroot-water mixture in a steady stream, stirring constantly until thick and clear. Pour the tofu-almond mixture back into the blender and add the agar mixture, blending well.

Spoon this in alternating layers with the Tofu Crème in tall wine glasses or champagne flutes, ending with a dollop of the Tofu Crème, and top with a whole strawberry. Chill for several hours before serving.

*Per serving: Calories: 352, Protein: 13 gm., Fat: 16 gm., Carbohydrates: 41 gm.*

# Tart Orange Mousse Cake

*Tart and light, a refreshing summer dessert after a rich dish such as pasta with pesto.*

Blend the tofu, sweetener, and orange and lemon zests until smooth and creamy. Measure the orange juice—there should be at least 3/4 cup. If not, add a little pineapple or grape juice to make 3/4 cup. Add the lemon juice, and dissolve the agar in it as described on page 10. Add to the tofu mixture, blend again, and pour immediately over the prepared Oatmeal Crust. Smooth the top with a rubber spatula, and chill until the top is firm. Decorate with Tofu Crème and fruits of the season. Chill completely before serving.

*Per serving: Calories: 341, Protein: 12 gm., Fat: 14 gm., Carbohydrates: 42 gm.*

Serves 8

2 lbs. silken tofu, pressed
   (see page 24),
   or 24 oz. extra-firm silken tofu
1/3 cup maple syrup, honey,
   or frozen concentrated
   pineapple or white grape juice
zest of 1 orange
zest of 1 lemon
2 large oranges, juiced
juice from 1/2 lemon
1 bar or 1 tsp. powdered agar

1 Oatmeal Crust, page 232,
   baked in a springform pan

Tofu Crème, page 218

Strawberries, kiwi fruit slices,
   blueberries, or other fruit in
   season to decorate top

# Italian Cheese-less Cake

*Serves 10*

1/2 cup sultana raisins

1/2 cup chopped almonds

1/2 tsp. grated orange zest

juice and grated zest of 1 large
  lemon

1 Tbsp. flour

26 oz. regular tofu, pressed
  (see page 24)

1/2 cup honey

3 Tbsp. rum
  or 1 tsp. rum flavoring

1 tsp. vanilla

2 Tbsp. arrowroot

1/2 cup sliced almonds

1 Almond Pastry Crust,
  page 234, patted onto the
  bottom of a springform pan

*This is similar to a cheesecake I had once in Italy that was full of raisins and nuts. I believe the original was made of ricotta and cream; this one substitutes no-cholesterol tofu to get very pleasant results.*

Preheat the oven to 350°.

Toss raisins, almonds, and grated zest with the flour. Blend the tofu, honey, rum, vanilla, and arrowroot in a food processor until smooth. Mix in the raisins and chopped almonds. Pour over the crust, sprinkle the sliced almonds on top, and bake for one hour.

Chill overnight before removing from the pan and serving.

*Per serving: Calories: 431, Protein: 13 gm., Fat: 25 gm., Carbohydrates: 38 gm.*

# Cashew Cheesecake

*This rich, creamy, no-bake cheesecake with an orange jelly topping was a favorite in my cooking classes.*

Wrap the tofu in towels and refrigerate overnight to remove the water. Mash.

Combine the cashews, water, lemon zest and juice, and in a blender or food processor and blend until absolutely creamy and smooth. This is very important or you will have a grainy cheesecake. You may need to blend in batches, then combine. Add the honey, vanilla, orange liqueur, and tofu and blend again until smooth.

Dissolve the agar in the orange juice as described on page 10. Add to the mixture in the food processor and blend again. Immediately pour this mixture into the prepared pie crust and chill in the refrigerator for 20 - 30 minutes.

When the top feels relatively solidified, prepare the orange jelly topping. Combine the orange and apple juices and dissolve the agar in it. Pour this on top of the cheesecake and allow to chill and set overnight in the refrigerator before unmolding and serving.

*Variation*: Use a berry or pineapple-base juice in place of the orange juice for the topping (the apple juice functions primarily as a sweetener).

*Per serving: Calories: 412, Protein: 13 gm., Fat: 20 gm., Carbohydrates: 48 gm.*

*Serves 8 - 10*

*1 cup raw, unsalted cashews*

*1/2 cup water*

*grated zest and juice of two*
*   lemons*

*1/3 to 1/2 cup honey (to taste)*

*1 tsp. vanilla, or seeds from*
*   1/2-inch vanilla bean*

*2 Tbsp. Grand Marnier or other*
*   orange liqueur (optional)*

*24 oz. regular tofu*

*1 bar or 1 tsp. agar*

*3/4 cup orange juice*


*Topping:*

*1/2 cup orange juice*

*1/2 cup apple juice*

*1/3 bar or 1/3 tsp. powdered agar*


*1 recipe Oatmeal Crust ,*
*   page 232, baked in a 9-inch*
*   springform pan*

# Tofu Crème

Serves 4-8

*Here are several versions of light toppings made from tofu. All of them can be used interchangably and you may find that you prefer one to the other. Although regular tofu can be used for any of these, you will find that the crèmes will be smoother and lighter make with silken tofu.*

**Basic Crème:**

1 lb. tofu, preferably silken

3 Tbsp. honey

1 tsp. vanilla

1 - 2 Tbsp. bland salad oil

1 Tbsp. Grand Marnier, brandy,
   or 1 tsp. vanilla

1 Tbsp. tahini (optional)

*Basic Crème:* Drain the tofu in towels by wrapping and refrigerating for 3 - 4 hours. Blend all ingredients in a food processor until thick and smooth. Chill before serving, if desired. Will thicken slightly upon refrigeration.

*Per serving: Calories: 127, Protein: 6 gm., Fat: 7 gm., Carbohydrates: 11 gm.*

**Tofu Cashew Crème:**

1/2 cup cashews

1/2 cup water

3 Tbsp. honey

12 oz. tofu, silken

*Tofu Cashew Crème:* Combine cashews with water and honey in a blender. Blend until smooth. Add tofu, drained as in the Tofu Crème recipe, and blend again until smooth.
Flavor as desired with vanilla, brandy, Grand Marnier, or lemon juice.

*Per serving: Calories: 126, Protein: 5 gm., Fat: 7 gm., Carbohydrates: 13 gm.*

**Tofu Coconut Crème:**

1 lb. silken tofu, pressed

1/2 cup coconut milk (freshly
   made or canned)

2 Tbsp. lemon juice

honey to taste

*Tofu Coconut Crème:* Blend the tofu with the coconut milk, lemon, and honey to sweeten until smooth and creamy.

*Per serving: Calories: 102, Protein: 6 gm., Fat: 5 gm., Carbohydrates: 3 gm.*

*Baked Apples Filled With Chestnut Purée, pgs 222-3*

# Oat or Brown Rice Crème

You would never imagine that whole grains could cook up into such creamy, sweet sauces.

Combine the oats or brown rice, apple juice, and tahini or nut butter in a large saucepan. Bring to a boil, then lower the heat, cover, and simmer for at least 20 minutes. Turn off the heat, add the remaining ingredients, and purée in a blender or food processor until smooth and creamy. If too thick, thin it out with more apple juice or soy milk.

*Carob Fondant:* The above recipe will transform into a healthy substitute for fondant, the sugary semi-hard icing on some cakes and petit fours. To the above recipe, add several tablespoons carob powder and a tablespoon of grain coffee substitute before puréeing. The amount of carob powder can be increased or decreased according to how "chocolatey" you want it to be. Delete the cinnamon and add the brandy. This can be poured over cakes or petit fours and will harden slightly, giving a smooth, slick appearance when chilled.

*Per serving: Calories: 145, Protein: 3 gm., Fat: 2 gm., Carbohydrates: 27 gm.*

Serves 8

1 cup rolled oats
   or cooked brown rice
4 cups apple juice
2 - 4 Tbsp. tahini, cashew,
   or raw almond butter
   (optional - for richer flavor)
2 tsp. vanilla
2 Tbsp. brandy or dark rum,
   or 1/2 - 1 tsp. cinnamon,
   or both
1 - 2 Tbsp. honey or maple syrup
   (optional)
up to 1 cup soy milk, if necessary

*Clockwise from upper left: Fresh Strawberry Almond Tart, pgs. 206-7, Lemony Lemon Cream Tart, pg. 228, Carob Walnut Kisses, pg. 235, Lemon Almond Wafers, pg. 238, and Spice Slices with Jam Dots, pg. 236.*

# Baked Apples Filled with Chestnut Purée

Serves 6 -8

See photo on page 219.

1 lb. fresh chestnuts,
   1 1/2 cups canned or bottled
   chestnuts,
   or 4 oz. dried chestnuts,
   cooked

1/3 cup soy milk
1/3 cup apple juice
5 - 6 Tbsp. maple syrup
 or barley malt
1 tsp. cinnamon
1/4 tsp. nutmeg
1/3 cup currants or raisins

6 - 8 crisp, sweet apples
a few tablespoons lemon juice
a little extra cinnamon

3/4 cup white wine
 or apple juice
1 stick cinnamon

1 recipe Oat or Brown Rice
   Crème, page 221
mint leaves and thin orange slices
   for decorating (optional)

*An entirely satisfying and warming dessert for crisp, cool, fall and winter days.*

If you are using fresh chestnuts, place them in a large pot with plenty of water and cook for about twenty minutes—the time will vary slightly according to size. Run under cold water, cut off the flat part with a sharp knife, and scoop out the meat with a spoon. If you are using canned of bottled chestnuts, heat them in their liquid (try to purchase a brand that does not use heavy syrup) until hot. If using dried, cook them according to the instructions on the package until tender (usually 20 - 30 minutes on the stove top).

Drain the cooking liquid and purée the chestnuts while still hot in a food processor or high-speed mixer with the soy milk, apple juice, 4 Tbsp. of the maple syrup or honey, cinnamon, and nutmeg, adding more spices if desired. Add the raisins by hand.

Peel the apples and remove the core from the top, leaving the bottom intact. Then, with a grapefruit or measuring spoon, scoop out most of the inner apple, leaving a 1/2" wall (strangely enough, measuring spoons with their thin, sharp sides work well for this). Chop as much of the edible scooped-out apple meat as possible, and add this to the chestnut mixture. Brush lemon juice onto the outside of the apples (to prevent discoloration), and sprinkle the insides with a little cinnamon.

Fill the apples with the chestnut mixture. Arrange the apples in a buttered baking dish, and pour around them the white wine, the remaining honey or maple syrup, and the cinnamon stick. Bake at 350° for 30-40 minutes, basting occasionally with the liquid in the pan, until tender. The liquid in the dish should be cooked down to a light syrup—if it seems watery, cook down on the stove over high heat until it thickens slightly. Pour this over the apples and serve. Pass a dish of the Oat or Cashew Crème.

Optional: To make this dish a little more elegant, the apples can be placed on individual croûtes. To make croûtes, trim 6 to 8 slices of bread, and cook both sides until browned in melted margarine in a skillet. Brush on the wine-apple syrup, and place an apple on each croûte.

*Per serving: Calories: 449, Protein: 9 gm., Fat: 5 gm., Carbohydrates: 91 gm.*

# Christmas Pudding

Serves 12 - 16

See photo on page 201.

1 lb. breadcrumbs, (about 5 cups)
    preferably whole grain
    (cake and cookie crumbs can
    also be used to replace part of
    the bread)
1/4 cup whole wheat pastry flour
1 - 1 1/3 cups currants
1 - 1 1/3 cups sultana raisins
1 lb. raisins
zest of 1 lemon
1 tsp. salt
2 tsp. mixed spices (cinnamon,
    nutmeg, allspice, cloves)
1/2 - 1 tsp. ginger

1/2 cup honey
8 oz. margarine
3 Tbsp. brandy or dark rum
    or 1 tsp. rum flavoring
egg replacer equivalent to 2 eggs
    or 4 Tbsp. tahini creamed with
    2 Tbsp. arrowroot and 1/3 cup
    water

*A real traditional once-a-year treat that is well worth the trouble. Serve with Brandy Sauce, Grand Marnier Sauce, Citrus Brandy Sauce, (pages 243-4) or unaccompanied. It keeps well, tightly wrapped, for many, many weeks, so it can be made ahead of time, if desired.*

Mix all but the last four ingredients in a large bowl. Cream the honey with the margarine and brandy, and work it into the first mixture with your hands. Add egg replacer or tahini-arrowroot mixture to bind all the ingredients. Pat the mixture into a well-oiled ceramic or metal bowl, cover with a double layer of aluminum foil, and place in a large pot. Fill the pot half-way up the bowl with hot water, cover, and simmer for 7 to 9 hours. Be sure that the pot does not run out of water—otherwise, you can pretty much leave it alone.

Allow to sit for at least 1 hour before inverting onto a plate. Pour some more brandy on it, if desired, and light it with a match as you carry it into the dining room. The flame will die down in moments, and alcohol will burn off, but this creates a spectacle. Slice, serve, and pass the Brandy or Grand Marnier Sauce, if desired.

Note: If you're making this several days or even weeks in advance, leave in the bowl and re-steam in the pot for an hour before serving. Let it sit for 15 minutes before inverting onto a platter.

*Per serving: Calories: 486, Protein: 7 gm., Fat: 15 gm., Carbohydrates: 83 gm.*

# Almond Cake

Here's a delicate, rich cake perfect for tea. The recipe can also be doubled to make two layers for a delicious layer-cake put together with an all-fruit, sugarless jam and covered with Tofu Crème, page 218. See the note below for making a Christmas Tree Cake with this.

Heat the oven to 350°. Grease and flour an 8" round cake pan, preferably springform or with a false bottom.

Cream the honey and margarine. Add the almond meal and okara. Sift the flour with the baking powder and add to the mixture, mixing gently. Finally add the soy milk and brandy, mixing gently but well.

Spread into the prepared pan. Cover the top with almond slices and bake for about 20 minutes. Allow to cool completely before removing from the pan.

*Christmas Tree Cake:* This batter is thick enough that it can actually be patted into any shape desired, e.g., hearts, triangles, etc. To assemble a Christmas tree-shaped cake that will delight both children and adults during the holidays, grease a large cookie sheet and flour it. Make double the amount of the recipe, and form two trees on the sheet (triangles with a square stump--better to keep it simple). Bake for twenty minutes at 350°. After the layers have cooled, put them together with an all-fruit jam. Make 3 recipes of the Tofu Crème, page 218, and to 2/3 of it, add parsley juice to color it a bright green (mince parsley in a food processor, and press in a thin towel to squeeze out the juice). Add carob powder to the remaining 1/3 of the Tofu Crème. Now frost the tree with the green crème, and use the carob crème to frost the trunk. Decorate with cranberries, and if desired, pipe some plain, white Tofu Crème around the borders. Very pretty! Try also making a Valentine Cake, and use your imagination to create various shapes for birthday cakes, etc.

*Per serving: Calories: 360, Protein: 8 gm., Fat: 27 gm., Carbohydrates: 24 gm.*

Serves 6 - 8

1/3 cup honey

1/4 cup margarine

1 cup almond meal (pulverized or ground blanched almonds)

1 cup semi-dried okara (see page 17)

2 Tbsp. flour

1 1/4 tsp. aluminum-free baking powder

1/3 cup soy milk

2 Tbsp. brandy or dark rum, or 1/2 Tbsp. vanilla plus 1 1/2 Tbsp. apple juice

1/2 cup sliced almonds (or more, if desired)

# Fruit-sweetened Carob Buttercream

*Fills and frosts one cake (about 2 cups)*

*This is surprisingly rich and sweet, although it contains no buttercream, margarine, or sweetener other than dried fruit. Although it is quite delicious, it is not an exact equivalent of a French buttercream; this has more earthy overtones. Good for frosting cakes, cupcakes, and brownies.*

*1/3 lb. dates, raisins,*
*   or figs (dried)*

*water - 1 cup or more*
*   as necessary*

*1/2 cup carob powder*

*1/4 cup tahini*

*2 tsp. vanilla*

*1 Tbsp. grain coffee substitute*

*1 Tbsp. brandy (optional)*

*8 - 12 oz. firm tofu*

Whip the dried fruit and water in a food processor to make a smooth paste. Add the carob powder and blend again. This should be a thick pudding-like consistency. Add the remaining ingredients, varying the amount of tofu according to how light you like it. Purée until smooth. It should be thick enough to pipe on decorations, but light and rich. A richer flavor can be obtained by increasing the amount of tahini.

*Per 3 Tbsp. serving: Calories: 92, Protein: 3 gm., Fat: 3 gm., Carbohydrates: 18 gm.*

# Fluffy Carob Orange or Mocha Frosting

*Although by no means low in fat, this is very smooth, light, and delicious.*

In a blender, combine the cashews, water, and orange juice (and orange zest if you are not using the liqueur). Blend until absolutely smooth and creamy. Add the oil a little at a time (almost drop by drop) while continuing to blend, until thick and creamy. Add the liqueur, tofu, and melted carob chips, and blend again until creamy and smooth. Chill briefly, then whip with an electric mixer at high speed until light and fluffy.

*Mocha Frosting:* Delete the orange juice, zest, and orange liqueur. In place of water, use 1/3 cup very strong grain coffee substitute or decaffeinated coffee. If desired, add 1-2 Tbsp. Kahlua.

*Per 3 Tbsp. serving: Calories: 140, Protein: 4 gm., Fat: 9 gm., Carbohydrates: 11 gm.*

*Makes enough to fill and frost 1 large cake, or frost 2 medium cakes.*

*1/2 cup cashews*

*1/4 cup water*

*juice of 1/2 orange*

*1/3 cup vegetable oil*

*12 oz. tofu, pressed (see page 24)*
*or 8 oz. firm tofu*

*1 to 2 Tbsp. Grand Marnier*
*or Cointreau,*
*or zest from 1/2 orange*

*1 cup carob chips (unsweetened non-dairy), melted*

# Lemony Lemon Cream Tart

Serves 8   (one 9-inch tart)

See photo on page 220.

scant 2/3 cup raw cashew nuts

3/4 cup water

grated zest of 1 1/2 lemons

1/2 cup lemon juice

2/3 cup honey

2 Tbsp. cornstarch, arrowroot,
   or 1 Tbsp. kuzu

1/2 lb. tofu

1 Tbsp. Grand Marnier or other
   orange liqueur (optional)

3/4 tsp. agar powder,
   or 3/4 bar agar

1/4 cup orange juice

1 baked tart shell of your choice

*Very zesty, creamy, and luscious.*

Blend the cashews with the water, lemon juice, zest, and honey in a food processor or blender until absolutely smooth and creamy. Remove all but 1/2 cup of this mixture, place in a saucepan, and heat over a gentle flame. When hot, dissolve the arrowroot, cornstarch, or kuzu in a small amount of water and add, stirring constantly until thickened.

Crumble the tofu and add it to the remaining 1/2 cup of the lemon-cashew mixture in the blender and process again until smooth and creamy. Mix this with the thickened mixture above and transfer to a large bowl. Add the Grand Marnier.

Dissolve the agar in the orange juice as described on page 10 and whisk well into the lemon-tofu-cashew mixture. Pour immediately into the prepared tart crust, and chill until firm. Decorate with thin lemon slices and Tofu Crème rosettes, if desired.

For Lemon Mousse, pour into wine or parfait glasses, alternating with fresh berries or other fruit in season and topping with Tofu or Cashew Crème, page 218.

*Per serving: Calories: 298, Protein: 6 gm., Fat: 13 gm., Carbohydrates: 43 gm.*

# Banana Cream Pie

*Serves 8*

*I created this for the diabetic father of a friend of mine who loved banana cream pies. Upon the first bite he exclaimed, "It isn't like the one they serve at Roy's Truck Stop; it's much better!"*

*This pie depends on the ripeness of bananas for much of the flavor, so be sure that they are really ripe. In fact, the riper they are, the tastier the pie, so use bananas that are covered with brown spots, the kind that you normally wouldn't eat. And that's the secret—otherwise, it's as easy as pie.*

Purée the bananas with the tofu, lemon juice, rum, and honey in a food processor until very smooth. Dissolve the agar in the juice as directed on page 10. Add it to the banana mixture in the food processor and blend for 30 seconds. Pour into the prepared Oatmeal Pie Crust and refrigerate until the top is firm, at least 15 minutes. Decorate the entire surface with the Tofu Crème and chill for at least 4 hours before serving. The topping will help prevent oxidation which leads to discoloration of the surface. Therefore, it is a good idea to cover the entire surface with rosettes or stars. Any discoloration that does occur will not affect the flavor of the pie.

*Per serving: Calories: 489, Protein: 17 gm., Fat: 19 gm., Carbohydrates: 62 gm.*

2 1/2 cups very ripe bananas,
    mashed (about 5 medium)

1 1/2 lbs. regular tofu, pressed
    or 1 lb. very firm tofu

juice of 1 lemon

1 Tbsp. dark rum
    or 1/2 tsp. rum flavoring

2 - 3 Tbsp. honey
    or frozen concentrated fruit
    juice, if desired

1/2 bar or 1/2 tsp. agar

1/2 cup orange or apple juice

1 Oatmeal Pie Crust, pre-baked,
    page 232

1 recipe Tofu Crème or Tofu
    Coconut Crème, page 218

# Pumpkin Pie

*Serves 8*

1 (9") whole wheat pie crust,
   unbaked

1 lb. cooked, mashed pumpkin
   (canned is fine)

10 oz. firm tofu

1/2 cup honey (or more to taste)

1/4 cup raisin syrup
 or 2 Tbsp. molasses (optional)

1 1/2 - 2 tsp. cinnamon

1 - 1 1/2 tsp. ginger

1/4 tsp. cloves

1/4 tsp. nutmeg

1/4 tsp. sea salt

2 Tbsp. arrowroot or cornstarch

1/2 tsp. grated orange rind
   (optional—gives it a less
   traditional but refreshing
   taste)

*Quite tasty. You won't miss the cream or eggs. Top with Tofu Crème or Tofu Cashew Crème, page 218, for a special treat.*

Blend all the ingredients until smooth in a food processor. Pour into the unbaked pie crust and bake at 425° for 10 minutes, then reduce to 350° and continue baking for an additional 40 minutes, or until the pie feels firm.

This is delicious either hot or cold. It can be baked several days in advance and reheated before serving, if desired.

*Per serving: Calories: 233, Protein: 6 gm., Fat: 8 gm., Carbohydrates: 36 gm.*

# Whole Wheat Pie Crust

*Simple to make and very tasty. Unlike most pie crusts, this one can be rolled out immediately or even patted into the pie tin.*

Mix the flour and salt, and stir in the oil with a fork. Add the apple juice and mix well. At first, it may seem very wet, but it will dry out almost immediately. Form into a ball and roll out between sheets of waxed paper or on a pastry cloth, or simply pat into the pie plate with your hands.

*Per serving: Calories: 115, Protein: 2 gm., Fat: 7 gm., Carbohydrates: 11 gm.*

*Makes 2 crusts*

*2 cups whole wheat pastry flour*

*1/2 tsp. salt*

*1/2 cup oil*

*1/3 to 1/2 cup chilled apple juice*

# Oatmeal Crust

*Makes 1 crust*

1 1/2 cups rolled oats

1/2 cup whole wheat pastry flour

pinch of salt (optional)

5 Tbsp. corn or safflower oil

2 Tbsp. honey or maple syrup

2 - 3 Tbsp. brandy, rum,
   or apple juice

*A sweet, crunchy, cookie-like crust that is great for cream pies and cheesecakes. And it's hard to mess this one up—very easy!*

Mix the oats, flour, and salt in a bowl. In a separate container, mix the oil and honey well. Add to the oat-flour mixture, and mix well. Mix in the liquor or apple juice, adding enough to moisten the mixture and hold it all together. Pat it into an oiled 9"- 10" pie tin or springform mold, as indicated in the particular recipe to be used. Bake for about 12 - 15 minutes at 375° until a light golden brown. Do not allow it to brown too much or it will be dry. The crust will become crispy as it cools.

Fill when cool.

*Per serving: Calories: 230, Protein: 5 gm., Fat: 11 gm., Carbohydrates: 28 gm.*

# Flaky Pie Crust

*Excellent for all pies and pastries, sweet and savory. The tahini replaces egg yolk in producing a rich crust that holds together well, making it perfect for Pâté en Croûte, pages 42-3.*

Combine the flour and salt in a large bowl. With a pastry cutter or a mixer on low speed, cut in the margarine to make little beads (the more you blend, the mealier and less flaky the crust becomes). Dilute the tahini with a little of the water, then add the remaining water and mix well. Add to the flour mixture and mix gently. Combine into a ball and chill for at least one hour before rolling out.

*Per serving: Calories: 134, Protein: 3 gm., Fat: 8 gm., Carbohydrates: 12 gm.*

*Makes 3 - 4 crusts*

18 oz. whole wheat pastry flour
   (approx. 4 cups)
1 tsp. salt
10 oz. margarine, chilled well
   and cut into little cubes
   (1 1/4 cups)
2 1/2 Tbsp. creamy tahini
chilled water added to tahini to
   make approximately 2/3 cup

# Almond Pastry (Almond Short Crust)

Makes 1 crust

3/4 cup whole wheat pastry flour

3/4 cup blanched almond meal
   or powder
   (this should be very fine)

pinch of salt

3 oz. unsalted margarine, chilled
   and cut into little cubes

1 1/2 Tbsp. honey

1 Tbsp. brandy or dark rum
   (or 1 tsp. vanilla and 2 tsp.
   water)

*Delicious as a crust for Strawberry Almond Tart, pages 206-7, and other fresh fruit tarts, as well as for cheesecake.*

Combine the flour, almond meal, and salt in a bowl. With a pastry cutter or mixer on low speed, cut in the margarine until it resembles coarse meal. Mix in the honey, and the brandy to hold it all together. Chill several hours or overnight before rolling out or you will have a sticky mess.

After rolling out, place in a lightly greased tin. Bake for 13 - 15 minutes at 350° and allow to cool before filling with pastry cream, custard, fresh fruit, etc.

*Per serving: Calories: 237, Protein: 5 gm., Fat: 18 gm., Carbohydrates: 15 gm.*

# Carob Walnut Kisses

*Rich and delicious without being overly sweet.*

Mix the margarine, honey, grain coffee substitute and the carob powder until well blended. Add the walnuts and flour and mix until completely blended, but do not overmix or beat. Pipe out into fat kisses on a greased baking sheet, then bake in a preheated 350° oven for 12 - 13 minutes. They will be very soft when they come out of the oven but will become delicately crisp as they cool on the rack. Store in an airtight container.

*Per kiss: Calories: 56, Protein: 1 gm., Fat: 3 gm., Carbohydrates: 7 gm.*

*Makes 40 kisses*

*See photo on page 220.*

*1/2 cup margarine*

*1/2 cup honey*

*2 heaping Tbsp. grain coffee substitute*

*5 Tbsp. carob powder*

*4 oz. walnuts, ground in a blender (1/2 cup)*

*1 cup whole wheat pastry flour plus 1/4 cup (optional—a little extra flour will produce a firmer cookie. The less flour, the more delicate these will be.)*

# Spice Slices with Jam Dots

*Makes 4 dozen*

*See photo on page 220.*

*1/2 cup margarine*

*1/2 cup honey*

*1 tsp. vanilla*

*2 1/3 cups whole wheat pastry
   flour*

*1 tsp. cardamon*

*2 tsp. cinnamon*

*1/2 tsp. ginger*

*1/4 tsp. cloves*

*1/4 tsp. nutmeg*

*1/4 tsp. allspice*

*approx. 1/2 cup sugarless,
   all-fruit jam of your choice*

Beat the margarine and honey until smooth and creamy then add the vanilla. Sift the flour with the spices and add to the margarine mixture. Mix well but do not overbeat. Roll into 1 1/2" logs and chill until they can be cut neatly. Slice into 1/4" slices. Make an indentation in the middle of each slice with your finger and fill with a half-teaspoon of jam. Bake in a preheated 350° oven for 7 to 8 minutes.

*Per cookie: Calories: 48, Protein: 1 gm., Fat: 2 gm., Carbohydrates: 7 gm.*

# Carob Chip or Carob Carob Chip Cookies

*The addition of ground walnuts to this recipe produces rich, satisfying cookies. Forget Tollhouse!*

Mix the margarine with the honey until smooth. Add the cinnamon and vanilla, then the walnuts, flour, and baking powder (either sift with the flour or mix into the flour well before adding). Add the carob chips and optional chopped nuts last, then bake in a preheated 350° oven for 10 to 15 minutes until golden brown.

*Per cookie: Calories: 72, Protein: 1 gm., Fat: 4 gm., Carbohydrates: 9 gm.*

*Makes 4 dozen*

1/2 cup margarine

3/4 cup honey

3 scant tsp. cinnamon

1 tsp. vanilla

4 oz. walnuts, ground in a
    blender (1/2 cup)

for Carob Chip Cookies:

1 1/3 cups whole wheat pastry
    flour

for Carob Carob Chip Cookies:

1 cup whole wheat pastry flour
    and 1/3 cup carob powder
    plus 2 Tbsp. grain coffee
    substitute

1 tsp. aluminum-free baking
    powder (optional)

# Lemon Almond Wafers

*Makes 4 dozen*
*See photo on page 220.*

*1/2 cup margarine*
*1/3 cup honey*
*1 Tbsp. tahini*
*grated rind of one lemon*
*1 Tbsp. lemon juice*
*2 1/2 cups whole wheat pastry*
*    flour*

*Topping:*
*4 Tbsp. honey*
*2 Tbsp. lemon juice*
*1 cup (approx.) sliced almonds*

*Delicate lemony wafers with the crunch of almonds.*

Mix the margarine, honey, and tahini until well blended. Add the lemon rind and lemon juice. Then add the flour and mix thoroughly, but do not overbeat. Roll into a log 1 1/2" in diameter and chill for at least two hours, preferably overnight. Slice 1/4" thick and place the slices onto a greased cookie sheet.

For the topping, place the honey and lemon juice in a small saucepan and bring to a boil for one minute. Remove from heat. Brush the slices with this mixture, then sprinkle generously with almond slices. Bake in a preheated 350°oven for 10 - 12 minutes until the almonds are golden brown and the cookies have spread out a little.

*Per cookie: Calories: 69, Protein: 1 gm., Fat: 4 gm., Carbohydrates: 8 gm.*

# Tahini Shortbread

I created this and the Honey-Soaked Tahini Almond Cakes in college when I tried to get the student co-op to order tahini. No one knew what it was or how to use it, so I had to convince a few people of its merits, then order about twenty pounds of it for myself in order to meet the required minimum. Then I had to create numerous delectable ways to use the stuff up! A teacher informed me a few years ago that my tahini recipes were still circulating within the co-op.

It is very important to use the very smooth, Middle-Eastern style tahini and not the grainy, raw type. Both are usually found in natural food stores.

Cream the tahini and margarine, then add the salt and honey, and mix thoroughly. Sift the flour with the cornstarch and add to the tahini mixture, gently mixing it in with your hands. Press into an 8" pan so that it is 1/3" to 1/2" thick. Bake in a preheated 325° oven for 15 to 30 minutes, depending on the thickness. Do not allow it to brown or it will become dry and crumbly.

*Per square: Calories: 84, Protein: 2 gm., Fat: 5 gm., Carbohydrates: 9 gm.*

*Makes 2 dozen squares*

1 cup tahini

1/4 cup margarine, preferably unsalted

1/4 tsp. salt (optional)

1/3 cup honey

1 cup whole wheat pastry flour

1/4 cup cornstarch or arrowroot

# Honey-soaked Tahini Almond Cakes

Makes 24 "cakes"

1 cup tahini

1/3 cup margarine

1/2 cup honey

1/4 cup almond paste

1 1/2 cups whole wheat pastry
 flour

1/3 cup walnuts, pecans
 or almonds, finely chopped

1/4 to 1/3 cup extra honey for
 sauce plus a little water and
 vanilla extract

*A Greek bakery in Santa Fe inspired these cookies, even though the original ones contained no tahini as far as I know. They are rich and sweet with an unusual flavor.*

Cream the tahini and margarine. Work the honey into the almond paste in a separate bowl, then add to the creamed ingredients. Add the flour 1/2 cup at a time, making sure that the dough does not become too stiff (a little less than 1 1/2 cups may be required). It should have some resilience. Shape into little oblong, flat cakes about 1 1/2" by 2 1/2". Press some chopped nuts onto the tops. Bake on a greased cookie sheet at 350° for 10 to 15 minutes until they are a delicate brown.

While the cookies are baking, dilute the honey with a little (2 to 3 Tbsp.) water. Add a little vanilla and heat over a low flame until the honey is completely dissolved. When the cookies come out of the oven, transfer them to a plate, then pour a teaspoon or two of the honey sauce on each while the cookies are still warm.

*Per cake: Calories: 113, Protein: 3 gm., Fat: 5 gm., Carbohydrates: 16 gm.*

# Sesame Raisin Balls

*Here's a quick one for the kids, hikers, sports enthusiasts and anyone who wants an energy-packed, delicious treat that can be whipped up in just minutes. A great addition to lunch boxes and for carrying "on the road" when hunger strikes and there's nothing but fast food joints in sight.*

Grind the sesame seeds in a blender or food processor to a powder. Remove and place in a bowl. Chop the raisins finely in a food processor or by hand with a sharp knife and chopping board. Combine the raisins, sesame seeds, and peanut or sesame butter and mix well. If the barley malt or brown rice syrup is fairly liquid, add it to the mixture as is. If not, heat in a small saucepan until liquid. Add the cinnamon and combine all. Form into little balls, roll in the desired covering, and enjoy!

*Per Ball: Calories: 82, Protein: 2 gm., Fat: 4 gm., Carbohydrates: 11 gm.*

*Makes 20 1" balls*

3/4 cup lightly toasted sesame
   seeds, preferably hulled*

1 cup raisins

3 Tbsp. peanut or sesame butter

3-6 Tbsp. barley malt, brown rice
   syrup, or honey

1/2 tsp. cinnamon

wheat germ, carob powder, grated
   coconut, or cookie crumbs for
   rolling the balls in

*If you cannot find toasted
   sesame seeds, dry-roast them
   in a frying pan over medium
   heat, stirring until they give
   off a fragrance and begin to
   crackle. REMOVE FROM
   HEAT IMMEDIATELY. Do
   not allow them to brown or
   they will be bitter.*

# Peanut Butter Cookies

Makes 36 cookies

1 cup peanut butter

1/3 cup oil

1/2 cup honey

1 tsp. vanilla

2 tsp. cinnamon

1 3/4 to 2 cups whole wheat
  pastry flour

1/2 cup currants or raisins
  (optional)

*I like currants in these cookies very much.*

Mix the peanut butter with the oil and honey until smooth
and creamy. Add the vanilla and cinnamon. Mix in the flour
and currants, adding a tad more flour if the mixture seems
extremely sticky. Drop by spoonfuls onto a greased cookie
sheet and flatten out with the back of a fork. Bake for 12
minutes at 350°.

*Per cookie: Calories: 91, Protein: 3 gm., Fat: 6 gm., Carbohydrates: 10 gm.*

# Grand Marnier Sauce

Makes 2 cups

*Serve this warm or chilled over cake, ice cream, or Christmas Pudding, page 224.*

Heat the orange juice and honey until almost boiling, then slowly add the dissolved kuzu or cornstarch, stirring constantly with a wooden spoon or wire whisk, until thickened. Add the milk and vanilla, heat for another minute, and finally add the Grand Marnier. Allow to cool slightly before serving.

*Per 2 Tbsp. serving: Calories: 55, Protein: 2 gm., Fat: 1 gm., Carbohydrates: 9 gm.*

1 1/3 cups orange juice
3 - 4 Tbsp. honey
2 Tbsp. kuzu
 or 3 - 4 Tbsp. cornstarch
 or arrowroot, dissolved in
 2 Tbsp. water
1/3 cup soy, almond,
 or cashew milk
1 tsp. vanilla
4 Tbsp. Grand Marnier

# Raspberry Sauce

Makes 1 1/2 cups

*A brilliant, deep red sauce that can be served with cake, ice cream, cheesecake, or mousses.*

Liquify the raspberries in a blender. Pour into a small saucepan—if you prefer, you can strain out the seeds by pouring through a sieve first. Add the honey and kirschwasser and heat. Add the cornstarch and cook until thickened. Serve chilled.

*Per 2 Tbsp. serving: Calories: 3, Protein: 0 gm., Fat: 0 gm., Carbohydrates: 6 gm.*

1 (8 oz.) basket fresh raspberries
 (about 1 1/2 cups)
2 Tbsp. honey
2 Tbsp. kirschwasser or brandy
1 - 2 Tbsp. cornstarch dissolved
 in a little water

# Brandy Sauce

Makes 1 1/2 cups

*Unlike the traditional sweet, buttery-rich brandy sauces, this is much lighter. Serve over warm puddings.*

1 cup soy, cashew,
  or almond milk

1/4 cup frozen concentrated apple
  juice

2 Tbsp. honey (optional)

2 Tbsp. kuzu,
  or 2 Tbsp. cornstarch
  or arrowroot dissolved
  in 2 Tbsp. water

1 tsp. vanilla

4 Tbsp. brandy or cognac

1 - 3 Tbsp. unsalted margarine
  (optional)

Combine the milk, apple juice, and honey in a saucepan and heat over a low flame, but do not bring to a boil or it will curdle. Stirring constantly, add the dissolved kuzu or cornstarch, and heat until thickened. Add the vanilla and brandy, and cook another moment. If desired, swirl in the unsalted margarine for a little extra richness.

*Per 2 Tbsp. serving: Calories: 34, Protein: 1 gm., Fat: 0 gm., Carbohydrates: 4 gm.*

# Citrus Brandy Sauce

Makes 1 cup

*Goes great with Christmas pudding.*

1/2 cup honey

1/3 cup frozen concentrated
  orange juice

zest of one orange and one lemon

2 - 3 Tbsp. brandy

2 tsp. cornstarch dissolved in
  1 Tbsp. water

Heat honey, orange juice and zests in a small saucepan. Add the brandy and cook for 2 - 3 minutes. Thicken with the dissolved cornstarch and cook for another minute.

*Per 2 Tbsp. serving: Calories: 92, Protein: Fat: 0 gm., Carbohydrates: 22 gm.*

# Mail Order Sources

In light of how difficult in can be to find unusual ingredients outside of major metropolitan areas, several mail order sources are listed here:

**Anzen Japanese Foods and Imports**
736 North East Union Avenue
Portland, OR 97232
503-233-5111
503-233-7208 (fax)

Sells a number of Japanese ingredients, including agar, kuzu, miso, rice vinegar, and dried shiitake. They prefer receiving orders through the mail but you can call for their price list.

**Chestnut Hill Orchards**
3300 Bee Cave Road
Suite 650
Austin, TX 78746
1-800-745-3279

Organic frozen peeled chestnuts. Because they're frozen they must be shipped by express courier (expensive). But if you want uncanned chestnuts any time of year, the expense is worth it--these are delicious!

**The Mail Order Catalog**
PO Box 180
Summertown, TN 38483
1-800-695-2241

Sells instant gluten flour, nutritional yeast, and tempeh starter.

**Mountain Ark Trading Company**
120 South East Avenue
Fayetteville, AR 72701
1-800-643-8909

An enormous catalog of ingredients and related cooking products. Many Japanese products available.

**Nature's Herb Company**
1010 46th Street
Emeryville, CA 94608
1-800-227-2830 (US)
1-800-523-5192 (California only)

Sells agar by the pound at reasonable prices.

**Now and Zen**
P.O. Box 591614
San Francisco, CA 94118

Sells dried okara.

# *Index*

## About Miyoko Nishimoto...

Miyoko Nishimoto, founder and owner of Now & Zen Bakery, is noteworthy as a vegetarian chef and jazz vocalist. Born in Japan to a Japanese mother and an American father, she moved to Mill Valley, California, with her parents when she was seven. Her bilingual and bicultural background has endowed her with the creativity and originality of the West and the aesthetic sense of the East in both cooking and singing.

Her interests in health and gourmet cookery prompted Miyoko, who became a vegetarian at the age of 12, to develop a new, dairy-free vegetarian cuisine. The originality of her healthful, tasteful, and very satisfying food style gained both industry and public recognition. Miyoko was soon teaching cookery, giving cooking demonstrations in department stores, developing menus for restaurants, and contributing articles on cooking to various national magazines.

She has opened Now & Zen Bakery in San Francisco, a company she hopes will change the course of dessert history. Now & Zen cakes, which look and taste very much like traditionally rich and elegant European tortes, are significantly different.

Miyoko has performed regularly as a jazz vocalist in clubs and hotels in and around Tokyo. In the San Francisco Bay area, where she now resides, she is continuing to pursue this career.

## *Other fine cookbooks from Book Publishing:*

These and books on Native Americans, midwifery, the environment, gardening, health, and lifestyles can be ordered from:

The Book Publishing Company
PO Box 99
Summertown, TN 38483
1-800-695-2241

Please add $1.50 per book for shipping and handling.